Men of the Rifles

Men of the Rifles

The Reminiscences of
Thomas Knight of the 95th (Rifles)
by Thomas Knight

Henry Curling's Anecdotes
by Henry Curling

The Field Services of the Rifle Brigade
from its Formation to Waterloo
by Jonathan Leach

LEONAUR

Men of the Rifles
The Reminiscences of Thomas Knight of the 95th (Rifles)
by Thomas Knight
Henry Curling's Anecdotes
by Henry Curling
The Field Services of the Rifle Brigade from its Formation to Waterloo
by Jonathan Leach

A LEONAUR ORIGINAL

First Edfition

Published by Leonaur Ltd

Copyright © 2007 Leonaur Ltd

ISBN: 978-1-84677-398-3 (hardcover)
ISBN: 978-1-84677-397-6 (softcover)

http://www.leonaur.com

Contents

Publisher's Note

This book brings together the writings of three men; two of them were Riflemen of the 95th and the other the was the chronicler of perhaps the most famous memoir by an old 95th man—Rifleman Harris.

The principal reason for publishing their words in single volume is, of course, their shared connection within one of the most famous British regiments of the Napoleonic Wars and, secondly, because individually these are shorter pieces which, without companion pieces, would have been unlikely to have found their way into print in their own right. We trust the many readers and students of the era will agree with us that the interest that exists and continues to be generated concerning Wellington's green sharpshooters makes every opportunity to expand the canon of the works that record their doings for the interest and enjoyment of the modern reader is one worth taking.

The first of our writers is Thomas Knight, an ordinary rifleman of the 95th and one whose name rarely, if ever, appears in accounts of the activities of the regiment or, indeed, in many bibliographies of its memoirists.

Knight saw action at the Battle of Waterloo and his account of the pursuit of Napoleon's French Army as it fled towards and into Paris in 1815 provides vital and interesting elaboration for those whose reading of the period have lead them to believe that the campaign concluded with the last shot at Waterloo.

Knight was at loose end at the close of the war against the French. His trade was that of a soldier and in keeping with many like him through the ages before and since, he cast around for another war and found one as a mercenary in Portugal supporting Don Pedro against the Miguelites. The cause or the identity of the enemy mattered little, Knight was a soldier—fighting in the company of other Englishmen in a British battalion and he fought for pay and subsistence—much, in fact, as had most ordinary British soldiers serving under the Colours of their mother country against a French enemy for whom they had held little personal antipathy.

Now known as the Liberal Wars, the British at this time ruled Portugal in the name of the absent king in Brazil, with Beresford effectively acting as Regent, until the revolution of 1820 when they were driven out and the king returned to the throne as a constitutional monarch. Knight recounts his experiences on campaign and upon the battlefield vividly. Given the location of his war and his background it is almost impossible not to read his exciting experiences as though they are a memoir of the Peninsular War. In fact, we might readily believe ourselves to be reading the further adventures of the famous Rifleman Harris himself!

This brings us to the anecdotes of Captain Henry Curling, who provided the pen for the words of perhaps the most famous British memoir of the Napoleonic period by a British soldier—Rifleman Benjamin Harris. Harris' memoirs have been available in several editions over the last century or more. The Leonaur edition[1] makes claim to being a complete version of Harris' story, only for us later to discover another book written by Curling which included—amidst his recollections of London Society and the theatre—more anecdotes of life on campaign during the war against Napoleon, including further brief recollections by Harris himself. These add only a smattering of new information about the soldier and shoemaker, but this book provides the perfect vehicle for bringing them to the notice of a wider audience.

The final piece in this book is somewhat different. It is a sketch—a history of the 95th(Rifles) from its creation to the Battle of Waterloo. What makes it special is that its author is none other the Jonathan Leach, who wrote a superb personal memoir[2] based on his own experiences, in the Peninsula and at Waterloo, as an officer of this famous regiment. This is, indeed, a personal take on a history by one who was a very active participant in its events.

We hope you will enjoy what we trust is a book—unique to Leonaur—which we further hope you will agree is aptly titled *Men of the Rifles*.

The Leonaur Editors

---

1. *The Compleat Rifleman Harris* by Benjamin Harris as told to & transcribed by Captain Henry Curling 52nd Regt. of Foot, Leonaur, 2006.
2. *Captain of the 95th* Rifles by Jonathan Leach, Leonaur, 2005.

The Reminiscences of
Thomas Knight
of the 95th (Rifles)

Contents

Preface

We fear that no one, who may read this, will regret the abandonment of our original intention to inflict upon him a disquisition on the subject to which the following pages chiefly refer; but we cannot refrain from expressing our opinion, that no man of unprejudiced mind (if such there be), recalling to his memory the circumstances connected with the assumption of the throne of Portugal by Don Miguel, can conscientiously and deliberately deny that this was accomplished by means, to say the least of them, *very indefensible.*

But stronger proof of this, than any we could adduce, exists in the fact, that the very men, then at the head of our own Government, (and who certainly cannot be accused of holding what are called "liberal opinions,") having the advantage of official information, denounced and treated Don Miguel as a perjurer and usurper, at the same time acknowledging Donna Maria as Queen, and, when occasion offered, paying her the honours usually accorded to Royalty.

How the same party have since been led to take this "perjurer and usurper" under their especial protection, is an enigma explicable only by witnessing the effects of virulent party and political feeling on the minds of men.

Were it a mere question, which of the individuals—Maria, Pedro, or Miguel—should be at the head of the Government, we should consider it a matter concerning the Portuguese alone, and unworthy of any honourable foreigner engaging in; but being the cause of freedom against despotism—of humanity and light against cruelty and darkness, and especially, being the commencement of that "war of opinion" (to use the expression of Mr. Canning) now spreading over the earth, every friend to the improvement of his race must regard the struggle with anxious interest.

That, among our own countrymen who have joined this enterprise, many have been actuated by the meanest and most mercenary sentiments, is undeniable; but we also know that others, disregarding the sneers, the intrigues, and the faintheartedness, both of foes and of friends, have devoted themselves to the cause, solely from sympathy with many brave men driven from their homes, and from an innate detestation of oppression and persecution.

History shows us that many of the noblest efforts of men have been darkened and almost disgraced by intrigues and the mean selfishness of individuals; and unfortunately the present can scarcely be considered an exception. We ought, however, to regard the object in view altogether independent of the instruments necessarily employed in its attainment; and although, in justice to these, we must express our astonishment at the perseverance they have displayed, and the difficulties they have surmounted, yet we are compelled to admit that their success is to be attributed quite as much to the infatuated imbecility and mismanagement of Miguel, as to any talent or wisdom hitherto displayed by themselves.

But, leaving the conduct of the political operators on both sides to be discussed by the historian, we have now much pleasure in introducing Corporal Knight—K. T. S.

A fortnight ago we never dreamt of becoming initiated in the mysteries *of proof sheets* and *printers devils;* but meeting Knight, and learning that he had lately arrived from Oporto, a spot to which we had for many months looked with deep anxiety, we were so much pleased with his graphic and animated descriptions of the various scenes in which he had been engaged, that we have been led to transfer them to the following pages, flattering ourselves with the hope of procuring for him a few pounds for his immediate support.[1]

Being quite conscious of our inexperience in writing, we begged for advice, and have received the following:

1. To exclude the greater part, if not all, of the Corporal's descriptions of eating and drinking, and getting drunk, &c.

2.. To infuse a little sentiment and fine feeling, on some occasions where it may be supposed natural, and to beg some professed writer to polish the whole.

3. Instead of giving only his own limited view of various occurrences, to concoct more full descriptions, and especially as regards the battle of Waterloo. Had we followed this advice, we doubt not that a more agreeable book would have been the consequence, as we cannot imagine that what Corporal Knight ate and drank, and how often he got drunk, can be generally interesting.

As to sentiment and tender feelings, they are what he has not the slightest idea of; and believing that, in books of a similar description, the characters of men in his station of life are usually altogether ideal, we resolved that, if this went before the public at all, it should be a true and honest history, such as we received it.

---

1. Since writing the above we have learnt, with much pleasure, that *all just claims* upon the Portuguese Government are likely to be discharged.

The whole has been formed from a confused mass of anecdotes and details, and our part has been to link these into a continuous narrative; and, whilst adhering to the Corporal's style and manner, to avoid, as much as was consistent with the reality, all disagreeable vulgarisms and descriptions.

In conclusion we beg, in justice to the Corporal, that, although he confesses to many iniquities, the reader will be so good as to refer to the certificates from his officers, and thereby convince himself that, notwithstanding all his plundering, drinking, &c, he deserves that character, which it seems to be his sole ambition to possess—*knowing his duty as a soldier.*

London
December, 1833

CHAPTER 1

I Enlist at Canterbury

My father was a cabinet-maker at Frome, in Somerset-shire, and, when I was very young, bound me apprentice to a weaver. Not liking such a quiet life, I ran off, when fourteen years old, to Southampton, and entered a Shields collier; but, returning from that place, we were driven into Ramsgate, and the cook boy and myself, being both tired of the sea and of ropes' ends, left our captain to cook his own dinner and to run his own messages, and set out on our travels.

On getting out of Ramsgate we were lucky enough to fall in with a return post-chaise to Canterbury, and it having no spikes behind, were carried along like gentlemen.

At Canterbury I was hired by one Tilbury, a grocer, with whom I remained for eighteen months.

This was in the years 1811 and 1812, when soldiers were much wanted, and being always a sharp sort of a fellow, fond of a frolic, more than one sergeant tried to cajole me, but it was of no use, till two Rifle Brigade men came to the town on furlough. Their green jackets and their fine stories were too much for me; so I agreed to join the third battalion of their corps, then at Shorncliff, near Hythe, under command of Colonel Wilkins, and gave my age as eight-een—although only sixteen, which was two years under the legal time. The next day I was taken to be sworn in at Hythe; having, as is generally the case with recruits, plenty of companions, as they are always flush of money for a day or two. The magistrate said:

"Well, young man, do you think you will like the army?"

"Don't know, sir; but I'll try."

"Well, whether will you go for limited or unlimited service?"

"What's the difference in money?"

"Limited is ten, and unlimited sixteen guineas."

"Well, sir, as I may never see the end of seven years, I'll take the sixteen guineas."

I suppose, from the way I gaped about at what the soldiers were all doing, they thought me a regular flat; and one old chap came up, and shaking me by the hand, said he was terrible glad to see me, for I was his *first cousin.*

"Yes," says I, "plenty of first cousins so long as there is shot in the locker; but I am not quite so green as to be done that way."

However, I soon fell in with jolly comrades; and in two hours had spent forty shillings out of the half of my bounty, which had been paid me; and, after having bought myself some necessaries, the rest of it went in two days more.

I was now drilled and put on guard. Being one night, from 11 to 1, sentry on the magazine, which I had been told that ghosts and such like used to haunt, I thought I saw something white, standing about six feet high; at first I was a good deal frightened, but taking courage, I fixed my sword to my rifle, and, creeping along, was about to seize it, when I discovered that it was the officers' leaping-bar, painted white. Some nights after this, the sentry, whose duty it was to be at this magazine, being afraid, told me he would treat me if I would stand sentry in his place, which I immediately did.

A young fellow, who enlisted at the same time as myself, asked me to desert with him, which I would not do. He was caught, and got the cat over his back.

The order was that all knapsacks should be filled with the men's kit, and hung up on pegs; but this same fellow was deep enough to stuff a pillow into his, and taking his kit with him, to leave us again, and to escape.

After being quartered hereabouts for some time, we were ordered to get ready to embark for Holland; and, being formed on a hill, five hundred of the ablest were picked out. As I was so young I was left behind; but the wife of one of the men making a great fuss about her husband going, I said I wouldn't mind to take his place.

The General, on inspecting us the next day, said it was not proper that I should go, as I was not able to stand the fatigue. He asked me who had selected me, and I told him I had volunteered in place of private Rook, who had a wife and family, and that I thought I could do well enough.

"Bravo, my lad!" said he, "we'll try you."

Two companies were then marched to Dover, where we rested for two hours, and thence proceeded to Deal, in all eighteen miles; this I found severe work, but did not let it appear.

As we were going out of England, we had a regular good spree this night; and, among other bits of fun, a pieman came in to the Deal Castle, where we were billeted. We bought and ate all his pies, shied the dishes at one another, and made the pieman drunk, and listed him.

His master came to get him away, but we made him pay smart-money for his pieman, which lengthened the treat. We embarked next day at Ramsgate, and our officer, in order to prevent anyone from walking ashore, planted a sentry on the quay. I was, however, resolved to get the better of him, so slipped over the side, and, swimming round, managed to get into the town; and on my return in the morning had a few hours' arrest for it.

Setting sail, we landed in boats on the left of Ostend, and before the last men were ashore, the first were quite uproarious with hollands—and the colonel, on falling us in, said he would work us for this.

We now got into canal boats, and the weather being excessively cold, were all more than sobered before reaching Ghent, in which place we were quartered for the night, in some old buildings. Next morning we marched, and after passing through some outlandish places, with odd names, arrived on the 13th day after landing, in the neighbourhood of Bergen-op-Zoom, to which place our army was laying siege.

While here, as the servant of one of our officers was coming from the rear with dinner, the wind of a round shot knocked him over, and his master seeing this, began swearing that he had lost it; the servant however rose soon after, and the officer got his rations.

The next night, whilst we were on reserve, the attack was made; but for some reason which I cannot explain, our troops, after having got into the town, were driven back, leaving many of our army prisoners. We were thankful when we got the order to retire from this place, as it was dreadfully cold stupid work.

CHAPTER 2

The Beacon

Retreating towards the Netherlands we halted at Courtrai, and then marched to Ypres, a strong place.

One evening, after the draw-bridge had been raised, a carriage coming to the gate, was allowed to pass, on bribing the corporal, and with the money the guard got so drunk, that on the field officer coming round, they could not obey his orderly's or the sentry's call, to turn out.

A fresh guard was sent for, and the others were tried by a court-martial, and sentenced to receive three hundred lashes each, tied to a tree on one of the public walks. The corporal, being tied up first, told Colonel Ross that he was a seven years' man, and in six months would not care for him or any other officer.

He, and the four next, took it all without uttering a syllable; but the other poor devil bellowed out, and climbed up the tree as far as the ropes would allow, begging for mercy all the time, but he got his allowance.

After all was over, the inhabitants cut down the tree, and would not allow any more to be flogged there.

After being quartered in several places, we marched to Dixmude, where we lay for about three months of the winter of 1814. There was a heavy snow on the ground, and Colonel Ross being no favourite, we one night collected an immense snowball, and rolling it up to the door of his quarters, closed it, and obliged him in the morning to get out by the back of the house. He laughed at the trick, but never afterwards was without a sentry.

At this place there were two nice girls at the shop, where we used to get our schnapps, and as they and I seemed to take a liking to one another, I managed to get a billet for their house, and they were very kind to me.

I used to assist them in all the little jobs about the house, such as serving the other men, cooking, and such like; and their cellar generally getting half full of water in the night time, I had to pump it out in the morning.

I had likewise to put a truss of straw round the pump over night, as the frost was so severe; but even with that it used to get frozen, and I had to thaw it with hot water before I could get it to work.

Our men and the townspeople were like brothers. One day we challenged them to have some sport with snowballs; they accepted our defiance, and we ranged outside the town.

Our men had collected a lot of snowballs in their foraging caps—proper hard ones—and we began the battle, officers and all. After a regular turn up we beat them into the town, and had famous fun in chasing them up and down—and *down* it was with many a one, as the snow concealing every thing, plump they went up to the chin in the ditches, roaring for help.

The windows had a bad time of it that day, and when it was over, the Colonel and officers offered to pay for those broken; but the townspeople would not hear of any thing of the sort, saying it was all in sport, and that as they had accepted our challenge, they would bear the whole expense.

We had afterwards several such engagements with the

inhabitants, and what with skating, sliding, and drinking schnapps, we spent our time merrily, and were very sorry to receive orders to march to Furnes.

Here another and myself were billeted on people who disliked us, and did every thing they could to make us uncomfortable, refusing us pans and other things to cook with, and by obliging us to use our canteens, gave us a pretty bit of work to make them look smart on field days.

Whenever I found the people civil, and desirous to oblige me, I was always careful to keep the places clean, and to give them as little trouble as possible; but we were so mad at those in this house, that we marched into the clean rooms in our dirty shoes, and bothered them in every way, till at last we forced them to pay us proper attention, and then we conducted ourselves as should be.

Adjoining the guard-room, in the marketplace, was a store-room for apples, and discovering this, we picked out a stone, and, with a fork tied to a long stick, we had always an excellent allowance, without buying them.

In the beginning of 1815 we marched to Menin, and our friends in England would now have seen the difference between a *home* soldier and one on service.

Not having had a change for two years, our regimentals were all in tatters, or patched up with every colour but white and red.

The first quarters I got into here were very bad, the people being sulky and disobliging; and on leaving them, my comrade got on a table and wrote on the ceiling with a candle, "D——d bad quarters for the 95th regiment."

Whilst here, our piquets lay in a village about; three miles off, separated from the French by a river, over which was a bridge. Our piquet house was in the market-place, which was covered in and surrounded with shops.

Besides ourselves there was a troop of the 15th Hussars, and also some Germans. The French and we were capital friends, the piquets going over on the sly to drink and chat with one another.

We were kept on the alert here, being called but at all hours, night and day, to prepare us for real alarms.

Remaining at Menin till the end of February, we marched to Louis, where we were brigaded with the 52nd and 71st.

The 2nd battalion of the 95th lay here, but our two companies of the 3rd battalion at Thorp, where we remained till 16th June, under command of Sir Frederick Adam—Captain Fullerton being my captain. Every Tuesday and Friday we had field days, and every Monday and Thursday the French had theirs on the same ground.

Our clothing was now so miserable, that I took up some of my pay that was due, to buy myself two pair of trousers and a pair of boots; but on the first field day, having several ditches to leap, I split my trousers to shivers, and next day the other pair went the same way, so I had to put on my old patched friends till I got one pair made out of the two damaged ones.

All had been a regular take in, for my boots, the first day I had them on, parted company with the soles, and I had to trudge back on my bare toes. After that I took care to leap gently, it being no joke to pay eighteen francs a pair for trousers, and to split them next day.

Once returning from field, a private fell out of the ranks, was picked up by the rear guard, brought to front, the brigade halted, and a drum-head court-martial formed in a field; but the man stating that his knapsack had been hurting him, the doctor was called, and it being found that what he had said was correct, he escaped punishment.

I was billeted at a farmhouse, near which there was a

cross, and many an evening have I gone down there to have a lark with the girls coming home.

The farmer with whom I stayed kept horses; and, at times, I assisted him at ploughing, and sometimes helped his wife at home.

On the night of the 15th of June, the sentry, on giving his orders up to me, said, "You are to keep a good look-out between these two trees, and when you see the beacon blaze up, you are to set fire to this."

As we were standing in the middle of a turnip-field, I said, "Set fire to what?"

"Why, to this."

"Oh, you gapus, what do you mean—set fire to a turnip-field?"

He was a half-witted fellow; but I found out by his winks and words that I was not to set fire to any thing, but to retreat to the guard-house, and give information when the beacon blazed. About one in the morning of the 16th, seeing a sudden light, I gave notice, and the officer of the piquet giving the alarm to the Colonel, the bugle was sounded, and we all fell in.

Getting permission to go and take leave of the people I was quartered on, the woman of the house filled my haversack with bread, cheese, &c. and I returned to the ranks.

CHAPTER 3

Mont St Jean

We immediately advanced to Tournay, and, passing through its long streets, rested for two hours, and then proceeded with a guide till about midnight, when he left us, giving the Colonel a route; but, missing our way, we came on a battery occupied by the French.

"*Qui vive?*" cried the sentry.

The Colonel now whispered to the Major, "We had better retreat;" and, accordingly, we ran back as fast as we could, they sending after us a round shot, which did no harm. We kept running for a mile, our canteens and sword-handles making such a rattling, that the Colonel gave orders to keep the canteens back with the left hand.

The Colonel and Major now consulted what was best to be done; and we were ordered to fall back on a village we had passed, and, knocking up the people to give us food and drink, halted for two hours.

We then advanced, about three o'clock on the morning of the 17th, and coming to a mill-stream, over which there was a narrow bridge, the Colonel called out, "You'll be all day in getting over the bridge; advance through the water."

I waited at first to get over by the bridge, but seeing my comrades in the middle of the stream, I leaped in also; the water was up to my middle, and, as I advanced, it became deeper, and seeing others of my height up to their armpits, I threw up my pouch, and putting my rifle over my neck, had a hard struggle to hold up against the stream.

After crossing it, we advanced up a lane, through a large wood, for two miles, the water running over our feet. We then came to a hard road, and turned to the left towards Brussels.

It was now about five o'clock in the morning, and in a little we passed and were cheered by our old friends the 52nd, lying down, half dead from fatigue; but our two hours' rest had greatly strengthened us.

Proceeding on to where the road turned off, about two leagues from Brussels, and marching towards Mont St. Jean, we passed over a meadow, where the French had bivouacked on the 15th, and our army having driven them back on the morning of the 16th, the ground was covered with dead and wounded.

Forming, about eleven o'clock, to the left of the wood, about a quarter of a mile from Mont St. Jean, General Adam ordered us to have some refreshment; and a bullock being brought, the commissary butcher killed and cut it up. We immediately lighted our fires, some having got wood, others the muddy water from the ditch close by, and hanging our camp-kettles, lost no time in cooking it.

As we expected something of the kind, it did not much astonish us when a volley came rattling about our ears; but being loath to lose our beef, some of which was done, and other parts quite raw, we tore off a few mouthfuls, and stuffing what we could into our knapsacks, were quickly ready to advance.

Great was our disappointment, however, to find that we had been disturbed by the Brunswickers, who had never seen the rifles before, and, from our dark uniform, took us for French; but being now on the move, we were marched into the village, through which it was scarcely possible to advance, owing to the number of wounded, wagons, carts, &c.

Halting here for half an hour, we were ordered to get out, as we could, in single files.

Leaving Fleurus to our right, at the bottom of the hill, we formed on the Brussels road, and then advanced towards that town, and passing the guards, came to within four miles of that place, and again turning to the left, reached nearly the same spot we had been at in the morning.

Whilst passing through the village of Mont Reveille, such a tempest of thunder, lightning, and rain came on, that from the slippery state of the ground our men were constantly falling, and our gaiter-straps breaking, the low shoes we had came off, and many of us had to walk in our stockings.

Our beds this night were a corn-field, and our coverings blankets soaked with wet; but some of us, setting out to forage, picked up wood, and making a blazing fire, we threw ourselves down beside it. Whilst foraging I got into a barn, and getting up to the loft, pitched down bundles of straw to my comrades. Oh, how comfortable I felt I could have made myself there, instead of going back to lie down in a splashing wet blanket on the ground.

On forming in the morning, my comrade said to me, "Whichever of us falls first, let the other have his kit;" to which arrangement I was quite willing.

We now advanced to the field of Waterloo, receiving orders to keep in the rear until we should be required in front, the Colonel at the same time telling us to keep well together; but there being just now little fighting, he allowed some to go back to the village to procure something to eat.

Getting into a large farm house, and finding one of the 95th dead, we supposed that he had been poisoned, and immediately plundered and smashed every thing there. We then filled our canteens in the cellar, and after stripping our dead comrade (who was no other than private Rook, in whose place I had volunteered) to the shirt, and wrapping him in straw, buried him in the garden, and divided his nice new clothes among those who were worst off.

CHAPTER 4

Waterloo

Falling in again we advanced to within a quarter of a mile of where the cavalry were making charges against the squares, and lying down behind a bank, remained here for some time to prevent the French coming up the lane upon our rear.

The wounded were now passing us in immense numbers; but neither they, nor the thunder of the guns, nor the rattling of the musketry, could prevent many of our men throwing themselves down and instantly falling asleep, so terribly were we knocked up by marching two days and nights with scarcely any rest.

The 52nd regiment having been engaged the whole morning, we advanced to cover them, and had much difficulty to avoid treading on the wounded, whose cries for help were grievous. The French, observing us to move, played upon us with grape and round shot, killing and wounding many, till we received orders to oblique to the right.

Getting into a rye-field on the right of the lines, we were immediately opened upon by the French columns, about 150 yards distant, and suffered severely.

About one o'clock we were ordered to advance and cover the 52nd lines, in extended files four yards apart, receiving orders, in case of being driven in, to form on the right of the 52nd, and the left of the light sub-division guns, and to fire in line until again told to advance and extend. We were obliged to fall back; and about half-past four o'clock, observing a large body of Cuirassiers half a mile distant, coming down upon us in close column to cut off our division, General Adam gave orders to his own brigade and to the artillery, to reserve their fire until they were within 100 yards, when such a volley was sent in among them that they were obliged to wheel round, leaving half of their number behind.

Word was now given to charge, and on we stepped, cheering and huzzaing, and, after a sharp struggle, we made the infantry retire, leaving many prisoners and guns in our hands. They took to the wood, but the 42nd driving them through, we ran along the sides, picking them up as they came out.

The 42nd were now in their turn charged by cavalry, and got terribly mauled. We were ordered to fall back, in order to lead the French after us, and this succeeding, wheeled right about, and charging, drove back those that had followed us. About seven o'clock, seeing large, dark columns coming up on our rear, we were afraid they were French, and that we should be taken prisoners; they, however, proved to be Prussians, which put us in high spirits, and, bringing our right shoulder forward, we advanced on the enemy, who, after standing it bravely for a little, took to their heels as hard as they could run, and never halted till they got to the rear of Fleurus.

Leaving them to the Prussians, those of us that remained, getting a little pea-straw, threw ourselves down, and never, before or since, have I had such a glorious night's rest. We had nothing to eat; but that we did not care about, being almost asleep before we had reached the ground.

Awaking early next morning, the 19th, we could scarcely believe our eyes, when we found that there were only six of us together. It was now, however, necessary to look out for provender, and seeing a large yard, with a lot of pigs in it, some Brunswickers and ourselves made a regular charge at them, and a famous bit of fun we had, slashing and catching at them.

While two of us made a large fire on the right of the Paris road, the others went foraging for bread and wine; we then demolished one of the porkers, drank our wine, smoked our pipes, and were as happy as kings. After enjoying ourselves for three hours, we set out in search of our comrades, and coming to some Brunswickers that we had seen at a distance, and had thought our men, were told by them that an officer and some of ours were more to the left, near to the road; on our discovering them, they immediately jumped up, and shook hands with us, so glad were they to see us alive.

Out of 205, the number in our two companies who had entered in the morning, 172 had been killed and wounded, five out of six lieutenants, and one captain killed, and one wounded. Two brothers, Lieutenants Shenley, of our company, were wounded, but both recovered.

Lieutenant Milligan, who was with the men, had already drawn rations, but went and got our allowance from the commissary, so we had more this morning than we could manage.

Whilst here, being ill off for firewood, one of the 52nd and 71st, followed by others, went with choppers to the bottom of the hill to break up a large ammunition-wagon, which the French had left; and, one mounting on the top, while the other was on the wheel, were chopping away, unaware of its being loaded, when a spark catching the powder, the 52nd man on the top was blown into the air, and the other was knocked to the ground, with one side completely singed. Hearing the report, we ran down, and lifting the poor fellow up, carried him to the doctor, who rubbed him with oil. Returning to collect the splinters, and looking about, I stooped down to pick up what I supposed to be a piece of wood, but was startled to find that it was a man's foot, all black with powder.

We then searched for the rest of the body, and discovered it all but one foot, and, it being an awful sight, we dug a hole, and buried it; we then demolished the remainder of the wagon.

Halting here this day and part of the next, we advanced to Paris.

CHAPTER 5

The March to Paris

We marched leisurely, refreshing ourselves with fruit of all kinds from the roadside; the potato fields also suffered, our swords and bayonets serving for spades.

One day, while foraging for garden stuff near a stream, a hare was started, and in a moment the whole of the Light Division was after her, and poor puss, taking to the water was followed by many, and caught in the middle.

Orders now came to the rear, where we were, to push forward by forced marches, as the French held two villages in front, strongly protected, and for two days and two nights we marched nearly forty miles a day.

About one o'clock in the morning of the second night we reached a hill, to the right of the road where our advance had been engaged the day before.

The French having been obliged to retreat into the village, we planted a battery on a hill, in order to drive them out; there being a vineyard down the hill, we cut down the vines, and fixing the supports and stakes in the ground, and plaiting the vine twigs through them, erected a substantial dyke, by filling it well up with mud, &c.

Not being so tired as the most of our division, I went to help the engineers, and being rather handy at plaiting the twigs, an officer observing me, remarked, that I ought to be with them, but to that I said "No."

After our battery had given them a couple of rounds, with little return, they retired from the village, and our drums and bugles sounding the advance, we entered, and found lots of wine, and rations all ready in their camp-kettles; and for some time it was impossible to get many of the men away from the meat and the wine, and, in the meantime, the French crossing the bridge, blew it up.

Our pontoons were some way down the river, and a part of the army falling back, marched to where they lay, and, crossing the river, came upon the French army, and at the same time the pontoons were brought up to take over the remainder.

Wherever we were, and whatever was to be done, we never let an opportunity pass of trying to fill our canteens and camp-kettles, and the place swarming with rabbits, we managed to catch some, and to get hold of a famous flitch of bacon in the village we had passed through. Near where we lay there was a mill, into which I, among others, entered, and getting in among the flour, filled my haversack with flour for dumplings.

My rifle uniform being all white, my comrades, on seeing me, called out, "Hello, miller, what's the price of the sixpenny loaf?"

"Faith, comrades, if I have a white jacket I have no white feather, and better be miller than be starved."

Running a chance of being shot if we went to the river for water, we had no help for it but to make our dumplings with wine, of which we had lots, and cooked the bacon and potatoes and everything in it.

Attacking the French we drove them toward the bridge, near the Bois de Boulogne; but, the passage being obstructed by trees, we made a number of prisoners.

The sappers and miners unyoking their horses, were not long in dragging away the trees in spite of all opposition. Getting over the bridge, we were stopped by an immense deep and wide trench cut through the road, and protected by a wall of wine casks filled with earth, topped by a *chevaux de frise*, and on each side of the road were fields and a wide ditch at right angles with the road; but none of these being defended, as they might have been, we had little difficulty in getting over them.

On our right we heard the Prussians rattling away, and, marching along, we reached the gates of Paris, and entered the town with colours flying and band playing. The inhabitants pretended to be very glad to see us, waving their handkerchiefs, and all that sort of thing, and passing through the Palais Royale, we returned the road we had come. The 2nd battalion of our corps was quartered at Montmartre; the 3rd battalion, in which I was, the 71st, the artillery, and some Cossacks, were posted on the right, and the 52nd on the left of the road from St. Denis.

A few days afterwards our division was ordered to stand in close column, while others were taking down from the Louvre, some of the statues and other things that Bonaparte had brought from other countries and placed there. From the sulky looks the people of Paris and the neighbourhood cast upon us, a row was expected; but seeing such a body of us, I suppose they thought it best to be quiet.

Many a curious scene we witnessed here, and many a bit of fun we had, more indeed than I like to tell. We used to be much amused by seeing the Cossacks, stationed beside us, strip themselves to the skin, and, unsaddling their horses, swim them into the Seine, now and then getting off themselves in the river, while their little shaggy brutes followed them: but one of them was drowned while at this sport.

Myself and two or three of our company nearly got into a scrape one day, as we were foraging in a field for vegetables. Finding, as we were busy digging, some musket-balls flying over our heads, and seeing a number of peasants busy loading and holding out at us, we immediately took to our heels, and being pursued by our enemy, made for a straw and mud wall about six feet high, in getting over which my foot caught the straw, and down I came on my back, and was soon overtaken.

I was in alarm about my bones, but they only made a great jabbering at me, and with their sticks, muskets, and pitchforks shoved me out of the field, and one of them gave me a rap on the back of the head with a pole, that made me see all the colours of the rainbow. This was too much to stand from Frenchmen, and meeting them sometimes in a quiet part of the road, coming with their carts to market, we used to set on them, and make their cabbages fly about.

As far as I have seen, whether in the British service or in the British battalion at Oporto, the constant look-out among the men was plunder, and to lay their hands on what they could, so long as they thought they should escape shooting or flogging; but here it was rather dangerous, as Lord Wellington would allow nothing of the kind, and more than one of our division were ordered to be shot for indulging these very natural propensities.

The first was one of the 52nd; but just as he was praying with the chaplain, an orderly dragoon galloped up between the squares, his horse all covered with foam, and announcing a reprieve, the man sprang about as if he were going to jump over our heads.

While here we had many grand reviews and field days, and on the whole had a very pleasant time of it; but there was nothing going on much worth telling about.

In October we marched from St. Denis to Versailles, and, while quartered here, our General's orderly having been despatched to Paris for orders from the Commander-in-chief, was attacked on his return by six Frenchmen; but as he was a big resolute man, he drew his sabre, and with it knocking down three, the others took to their heels. Soon after he was made sergeant-major.

CHAPTER 6

Return to England

We left Versailles in the beginning of the year, and reached Dover in February. Nothing happened of any importance during the march. On landing we were marched to Shorncliff, where we lay for a month to refit, and were then sent to Ramsgate to embark for Ireland.

My adventures are now very little worth telling.

We remained for two years in Dublin, from thence we went to Queen's County, where we had enough to do in hunting out stills for six months, and on the general reduction I got my discharge, on the 20th of November, 1818, and am proud to say that along with it I got a very good character.

Thinking I might as well go to Frome to see if any of my friends were alive, I embarked at Dublin for Bristol; but, being driven into Milford Haven, preferred walking over the Welsh hills, and, after a dangerous journey through the snow, got to Bristol.

Going from thence to Frome, I found almost everybody dead. I first worked as a country labourer thereabouts, and in Kent; afterwards worked here in excavating the St. Katherine's Docks and the London Bridge, and when these were finished went down to Chatham, where I first heard people speaking about the plan of driving away Don Miguel, and of putting Don Pedro, or his daughter, in Miguel's shoes.

On Saturday, the 22nd of October, 1831, when at Chatham, I was told for the first time that settlers were wanted for the Brazils, or elsewhere; and as I was now tired of quiet work, and wanted to have a little of the old game, I immediately went to the White Hart, where I was told I would learn particulars.

On going there I saw Captain Moss, who told me to come on Monday, when he would engage me. I did so; and, on seeing me, he said, "An old soldier?"

"Yes, sir; I was in the Rifle Brigade."

He asked me if I would like to go to the Brazils, and to be a militia man for a year.

I told him I did not care where I went, or what I did; but that I thought he wanted me for the young Queen that people were speaking about.

"Well," says he, "you're right; but keep it to yourself."

He told me he would make me a Sergeant; but I said, "No, no; I am no scholar, I would rather be a private." He gave me a shilling and a pot of beer, and another shilling from himself, and said he would allow me a shilling for every good man I got him.

I picked up twenty-three, but never saw the allowance; and for six days never had a sixpence of pay. The men that I engaged I used to blarney, by telling them that they were all going to be made officers and gentlemen, and all that sort of thing, and the flats believed me.

On the 9th of November we received a shilling each, and got orders to leave Chatham for the Isle of Dogs. We had to find our own food, &c. out of the shilling; and, on arriving at Woolwich, I sold my shirt for eighteen-pence, to get myself a bed and supper.

Next morning we reached the Isle of Dogs, where we

had plenty to eat and drink, and a big fire, and snug beds. We were here for three days, but the Miguelites in London hearing of us, and that the transports, the *Asia, Congress* and *Juno*, were lying ready to take us off, managed to get the "broad arrow" put upon them, and sent down from Bow Street to catch the officers, and to disperse us.

Captains Moss, Gray, and Steward were forced to decamp from the house, and a great many of the men went away for good. Captain Gray said, "Never mind, boys, if they knock us up here, we'll soon get the better of them in London."

I had not a copper, and had no place to go to in London, but had made up my mind to stick by them, and to take my chance of what would turn up, and was only afraid of being obliged to go home again. Walking along London Bridge, I met Captain Gray, who shook me by the hand, and said, "Well, my lad, I am glad to see you in London."

I repeated that nothing would frighten me from sticking by what I had once begun to.

I got into lodgings in Bishopsgate Street; and the next day, according to his orders, I met him at eleven o'clock at the Spread Eagle, Gracechurch Street. He gave me a shilling, and told me he would give me a shilling a day if I remained in London. He gave me a note to deliver to Captain Moss, who lived in Aldgate, and who gave me eighteen-pence.

I now wandered about London for ten days; getting but little food, and seeing no chance of any thing turning out of the affair, I had half a mind to go back to Chatham, I have been well used to starvation since that time, but then I could not stand it, and pawned every thing I could for a living, even to my Waterloo medal.

But now I heard that Captain Sinclair (Staunton) was collecting men, and soon found him out. He had got about twenty; but one day when we were all there, the police came upon us, and Dr. Souper, the examiner, was forced to jump out of the window to get clear of them.

They came to us, and said, "What do you men want here?"

We answered, "Waiting to see a gentleman." And were told:

"Come, be off, you ragamuffins, we know you well."

We now heard that Major Williams was engaging men in Great Windmill Street. I went there; was examined, and passed. They asked me here if I knew what was the matter in hand. I said I had a pretty good guess, having been engaged before in Chatham. They told me to try to get them some good men, and I did my best. Although we had all a pretty good notion that we were going out to Portugal, to fight for Pedro and the young Queen against Don Miguel, the word "soldier" or "fighting" was never mentioned by those who engaged us, and we were called settlers going abroad.

Every day we expected orders to embark, and several times we got a shilling to pay for our night's lodgings, and a ticket to receive another on setting off the next night, and many a one got the shilling who had no intention of going out; but it was impossible to judge who were true, and who were not. The Miguelites had also sent spies among us; all which obliged the officers to keep a very sharp look-out for themselves, and even with that, I have heard that some of them were taken up, but there being no law to hold them they were let off.

At length, on the 15th of December, we were told that all was ready; and at four o'clock in the afternoon, about a hundred of us were led off from our rendezvous, in small parties of ten men, each under the charge of what was called a "careful man," with a bit of white tape round his arm, through lanes and narrow passages, towards Vauxhall Bridge.

Here all the men who had engaged with other officers assembled, and, after a deal of noise with the women, and others who had followed us, we got into large barges, in which we were to float down during the night to the ship, near Gravesend, and received orders to keep ourselves quiet and off deck.

As I had had a good feed during the day, I was not hungry; but many having had nothing to eat for two days, when bread, and cheese, and beer were ordered, they seized it, so famished like, and tumbled over one another at such a rate, some seizing the share of three, and others getting none, that sitting, as I was, as happy as a king, smoking my pipe, I got many a good laugh.

About four in the morning we reached the *Edward*, off Greenhithe, and now some shabby scamps, after having got their shillings and their meat, refused to ship. I believe I was the first that climbed on board. We mustered about two hundred.

About six o'clock eight or ten officers came on board, having been piloted to the river-side by an old smuggler, who had been the chief hand in getting us all slyly off.

It was now I first met my future commander, Captain Shaw.

He came up to me, as I was leaning over the gunwale, and said, "Aren't you an old soldier?"

"Yes, sir."

"What regiment?"

"The old 95th Rifles."

"Know Colonel Fullaston?"

"Captain of my company, sir."

"Where have you served?"

"Holland, Waterloo."

He told me he had been in the 52nd, and brigaded

45

with us in Holland and at Waterloo, and after asking me a number of questions, to see that I was not gammoning, he took a great liking to me, and many a roasted potato and other necessaries of life I got, for having been one of the old Light Bobs, and he afterwards made me the right-hand man of his company.

We now went down the river, dropping anchor off Margate, to wait for orders where to proceed.

CHAPTER 7
Strange Doings

We moved over to the coast of Holland, keeping clear of the English fleet, and on the 21st anchored off Flushing—a good sized town, lots of steeples and whitewashed houses; two windmills close to the town also white.

We were no sooner there, than two Dutch gun-boats were laid alongside of us, and a guard placed on shore to prevent our landing or moving without leave. The weather was desperately cold, and we could not get out to have a slide. Ever since we came on board, many had done nothing but fight, riot, and mutiny, and Captain Shaw, who was very active in trying to keep them in discipline and in good humour, one day got both his eyes nearly closed, and never afterwards went without two brace of pistols in his pockets and under his pillow.

On Christmas-day we had a feast, and managed to get some gin from a boat, with which many of the men got very drunk and obstreperous. We had a bit of pudding—it was all dough—the plums were all in one place. Another day we had pork and pea-soup; the chaps all crowded round the coppers, scraping them and getting their faces as black as sweeps.

On the 27th of December we left Flushing, and, after a very stormy passage of six days, arrived at Belleisle in

France. On our arrival the men in the other ships gave us three cheers, which we returned; and Colonel Hodges came alongside, and asked the Captain, "How many on board?"

"One hundred and ninety-nine."

"Why not bring another man to make up the two hundred?"

The Colonel then called out, "How are you, men?"

Some of us old hands sang out, "All well, sir."

We were now ordered to be drafted into other ships, and in the meantime had slops served out: a pair of canvas trousers, a frock, striped shirt, a pair of shoes and stockings, and foraging cap; also hot water and soap—much needed—had a regular good wash, the water after it was as black as soot. Several of us agreed to have a rope tied round us and to have a duck in the sea.

We had our choice of a ship, and I chose the biggest, which was the *Rainha*. We were to serve as marines, and were commanded by Major Lawson and Captain Steward. We fell in, and were inspected on the quarter-deck. I was nearly on the right of front rank, and heard the officers say, looking at me:

"That is an old soldier from his actions;" for I had been showing the men how to fall in.

Major Lawson said to me, "Haven't you been in the army before?"

"Yes, sir."

"In what regiment?"

"95th Rifles."

"I appoint you corporal."

"I am very much obliged to you, sir, for the offer, but I'd rather you would appoint someone else, for I am no scholar."

"There is not much of that wanted, and I require old soldiers like you for non-commissioned officers."

But I refused it altogether.

A man, John Burn, an old pensioner of one shilling a day, next me, said, "I sha'n't be one, either."

The Major went down the front, came up the rear, and up the front again, and asked me why I would not take a corporal's place.

"Sir, I had rather be a private."

He then said to Burns, "You have been a soldier."

"Yes, sir."

"Will you be a corporal?"

"Yes, sir." So he was a double-faced fellow. The Captain then fell out those whom he had picked for sergeants and corporals.

We were then ordered below, and had hammocks and other comforts served out; but it was good fun to see the young hands getting into them; although some gave the sailors grog to show them how to sling them, and to get out and in, others would not, and many a bloody nose and cracked crown was the consequence.

We now lived like fighting-cocks, and had famous larking in all sort of ways. Messes of thirteen were told off, with a sergeant and corporal in each, and the order formed in which we should be the cooks of the day, whose duty was to clean the berths, and to bring down the rations cooked by the ship's cooks.

At eight we had our cocoa; at twelve, dinner; at half-past twelve, grog; at four, tea and grog; plenty of biscuits at other times.

We had often good fun, when the sea gave a lurch as the cook with a kid of soup was on the stair, seeing both come down by the run. We had also a trick of soaping the stair, which threw the head where the heels should have been.

A week after arriving at Belleisle, the paymaster came on board to pay the ship's company and ourselves, at the rate of £2.5.0d a month. I got £4.10.0d, two months' pay, less three francs kept on promise.

Nine of us getting two days and two nights' liberty, resolved to have some sport ashore, and to spend all our money; but soon getting top heavy, and the *gens-d'armes* finding us reeling about after eight o'clock, we were smacked into the police office for the night

Next morning one of us said, "I'll break the bar if you'll follow." I said I would. With this one picked up a big stone, and hitting the bar, snapped it in two, as it was old and not thick. We all scrambled out, and took our morning of good brandy in the town.

We were marching along to get some breakfast, when our officers seeing us half drunk, and threatening to knock down anyone who would interfere with us, came up, and, with the help of the *gens-d'armes*, got us into the boat, and on board.

I was greatly distressed that I had not spent all my money, and because I had been taken on board before my time was up, seeing it would be the last spree I was likely to have; however, we managed to carry four bottles of brandy on board with us.

On getting alongside, someone called out, "Glad to see you so obliging as to come back so soon, as it is now our turn."

I said, "Mind you don't get into their jail."

"Were you there, Tom?"

"Ay, for one night; but I am sorry my leave has been stopped by this here."

Next morning got up three parts drunk, and marched

as I could to quarter-deck. Major Lawson said, "Knight, I recommend you for coming on board sober."

Well, thinks I to myself, you are a pretty judge of horse-flesh.

"Now," says he, "all go below."

"Yes, sir," says I, glad to get out of his way, to have a snooze, and get sober.

Some time afterwards, as I was standing a-midships, near the gangway, Major Lawson came up to me and said, "What sort of a lark had you on shore, soldier?"

I told him I had got drunk, and was put in the cage. He said it was all right to get rid of my money—"Have you any left?"

"Yes, sir; but I wouldn't, if they had not brought me on board."

"Well, well," says he, "in four or five days you will have another day."

"That 's poor hope," says I, "for we won't be here so long, I fancy."

It was here that Mr. Jones, a midshipman, fell off the yards, just as I had gone below; he fell against the capstan, broke his thigh, and will be lame for life. About the same time, our first lieutenant's son was drowned while rowing between two ships.

On 10th February the whole fleet left Belleisle, and met with stormy weather. One day, at 4 p. m., whilst at tea and grog, a heavy squall came on, carrying away our topmast. All hands were piped on deck to help in clearing away, and in rigging a new one.

When this was done, I had seated myself in a bushel-basket near the galley fire, the ports were open, and the water coming through in full swing, carried me in the basket, from the galley, between two guns on the larboard. I just jumped out of the basket, and ran back to the galley fire, resolved to finish my pipe.

From eight to twelve, I was sentry on the scuttle-butt, to prevent waste, and to strike the bell, and from the way I made it sing out, they used to know when I was there.

The pitching of the vessel made the eighteen-pounders drive against the beams at such a rate, that the pilot told Admiral Sartorius that he must throw some of them overboard to ease the ship; but the Admiral flew in a passion, and said, "What are you afraid of?—Don't you know we have British sailors on board?"

We shortly afterwards sent this fellow to the right about and got another.

The water was now running from one port to another, across midships, and I was forced to hold on the scuttle-butt. The pumps were going all night Being relieved from watch at twelve o'clock, a Portuguese officer asked me to lash his two boxes together, as there was so much water in his cabin that they were knocking one another to pieces.

Having done this for him, he told me to find some grog that was in a bottle near. I found it, and making myself as wet inside as I was out, I did not care for any thing.

One day I was sentry forward to prevent the men lighting their pipes at the galley fire, while the Emperor and Admiral's dinners were cooking, and to keep them from troubling the sick.

Captain Steward came up to pass me; I said, "Stop, sir."

"Do you know your duty?" said he.—No reply. This he asked me two or three times, but I never answered. He went and brought the sergeant of the watch, and said to him, "What do you think of this fellow?" and added, "Give up your orders." I still kept silent He then said to the sergeant, "This is a fool."

At this I asked the sergeant, "Don't you know that it is *your* duty to say, 'Give up your orders to the officer,'—the officer himself has no right to ask me."

The sergeant said, "I believe you're right;" and then added, "Give up your orders."

"All right," said I, knowing my duty as a soldier. I then gave up my orders. The officer walked away, but came again in a little, trying to find fault, but I was too knowing for him.

A short time after this, whilst standing sentry aft on the quarter-deck, on Mr. King's stores, and to keep men from walking above where the Emperor was, Captain Steward came round with the sergeant in his watch to see the sentinels. On observing me, I overheard him whisper to the sergeant, "Oh, that's Knight; he knows more than we do: come on."

We were always on good terms afterwards.

CHAPTER 8

I am Made Corporal

After cruising about, taking some prizes, one a brig laden with bones, which we sent into Terceira, we reached that island, passing St. Michaels, which saluted us with twenty-one guns, receiving the same in return. We anchored before Praya; Don Pedro now landed, but we remained on board for a week, when the whole of us (about 400) went on shore to be drilled and formed into companies.

Major Lawson wanted to keep me, but Captain Shaw being appointed to the light company, and having selected me as an old Rifleman, I preferred going with him, as the right-hand man of the company; and as, on the whole, I had conducted myself pretty well, was asked to become Corporal, but again refused.

I was sentry on Colonel Hodges' door, when Captain Ramus and Captain Hill went past to shoot; they had gone over the hills, and separated in a thick fog.

Captain Hill coming home alone, it was feared that Captain Ramus was lost, and lights were got to search for him, and after a most dangerous night's work amongst the rocks and precipices overhanging the sea, he was found early next morning lying dead between two rocks, and his dog by his side. It was at first supposed that he had been thrown down, as the watch and steel guard which he had, were not upon him when found; and the men of these islands carrying poles, twelve feet long, nothing would be easier than to give a man a rap on the back of the head with them. But it was afterwards believed that he had, during the fog, missed his footing and tumbled down.

We carried the body home, and picking out old soldiers to give him all military honours, we buried him in the fort—the sick and every one following, he was so much liked.

We had now constant drilling, and I will say of the light company, that though I was the only old soldier in it, it could in a very short time go through its motions in a way that no regiment in the British service need be ashamed of. Excepting myself, they were almost all under twenty-two or twenty-three, but real good boys, as they showed in fight, over and over again—and now, of the whole of us—officers and men—who first embarked, there are not above sixteen alive!

One day Don Pedro with his aides-de-camp reviewed us, we cheering him, and he returning the salute.

We went through all our manoeuvres—formed line—square—fired by sections—from right to left and from centre to flank—broke open column by rear of light company—formed line to retire—halted—right about—charge, double quick, &c. &c. We then ran in companies to the fort in which Colonel Hodges was quartered, and past which the Emperor must go; afterwards retiring to barracks, we had double allowance of wine.

17th April. We got paid up to this day. I carried the sack full of money for the company down to the Captain's quarters, he walking with me—it was a regular load. The Captain told me to lay it down and rest, for which I was very thankful, and was still more so, when I had fairly put it down in his quarters: he gave me a few shillings.

Next day I got a pair of wings to make my coat look smart, and having to parade on Sunday, gave a man something to drink, that he might comb them and trim them up; but the scamp got drunk, and I had to appear on parade and at church with them, the only part of my dress looking ill.

Colonel Hodges used to preach every Sunday. He looked along the ranks, and, as I thought, at my wings, which made me afraid of getting extra guard.

He came past me, and said to Captain Shaw, "What sort of man is that on the right of your company; I have remarked him as very steady, have you any fault?"

"None."

"Then, I make him Corporal;"—so instead of getting two extra guards, I got two stripes.

There were certainly a number of very unruly fellows among us, and Colonel Hodges did not spare their backs. One day while an Irishman was getting his 200, from which he never flinched, another Irishman called out from the ranks, "Well done, Irish!"

"Oh, ho," says the Colonel, "wait a little, and we'll see how you like it, and instantly forming a drum-head court-martial, he was tried, and got 150, which he stood as well as his countryman.

One day on parade, a fellow who had been discharged from the fleet for bad conduct came to offer himself as a soldier; but the Colonel, knowing him well, called out, "Men, here is a blackguard who wishes to join you; if you duck him, I shall say nothing."

Upon that, piling arms, we seized hold of him, and, carrying him to a pond in the town, gave him a famous drenching, and then drummed him out; but the same night he came to the grog-shop, where myself and others were, and begged for something to help him on; we did give him a trifle, but next morning finding him lying dead drunk on his face, Captain Shaw ordered us to apply our straps to him till we made him roar. He was then marched with a file of men three miles out of town, and, being left there, we never heard more of him.

For about six weeks we remained at Praya, drilling for four hours every day, and practising all sorts of rifle and light infantry exercise, with which our Captain was well acquainted, and always put us through himself. After working away for some time he often said to me, "Knight, you may fall out."

So I sat down on a wall like a gentleman, and amused myself looking at the awkwardness of the young hands.

On 1st or 2nd of May—a regular wet stormy morning—we got orders to march to Angra, and if it had not been for the fun we had seeing the band with their fine white state dresses getting so drenched and dirty, it would have been a miserable day's work. For my own part, I had enough to do in getting two drunken men to keep up. Sometimes they would lag behind, and again they would take a run and get half a mile in advance. I think if it had not been for some grog I luckily had in my canteen, I should never have got them along; but by holding this out, I managed to coax them.

The Captain was afraid I should get drunk myself, and said, "Are you all right, Corporal?"

"Yes, sir."

"Well, we are coming near the town, take care and don't disgrace yourself and me."

My shoes, which were none of the best, dropped their soles, and my feet getting all blistered, I was in a pretty state, so to comfort myself I went into a wine-shop and had two pints of wine, and afterwards went down to the water-side, where I had a famous spree that night.

The next day, getting orders to embark, I got my shoes mended, receiving money to pay for them from the Captain, who at the same time said, "Now, mind you keep yourself sober."

He was always telling us to refrain from drinking, and great occasion there was for it, as most of us were fond of a drop; but I can say that I always kept myself clear of it, when there was any chance of duty to be done.

After getting on board, we were some hours without rations; but, luckily for me, I had put some wine in my canteen, and hearing the ship's cook say, "I wonder if the soldiers have any grog with them?"

I thought to myself some good was to be done; but, seeing the Captain looking if any of the men were tipsy, I said nothing at the time.

However, giving the cook a wink, he came up to me, and I said, "Wilt have a drop?"

"Let's have a drink," said he. "How terrible good it does taste. The ship's dinner will soon be ready, and you'll have some, Corporal."

On that I replied, "Wet t'other eye, cook." So I had a dinner, while the rest were waiting for their rations; and even when we got them, my friend the cook was very serviceable by losing no time in putting them in the ship's coppers.

We now cruised about in the *Rainha*, and being off St. Michaels, received orders to land and be reviewed; we consisted of about 6000 men, and the British were much noticed. On retiring, we had to cross a ditch, into which some of our men fell, but luckily without being observed by the Portuguese.

Orders were now given for the whole army to embark on board the squadron for Portugal, and we accordingly marched to Angra, where we had to wait five hours on the quay, before the boats came to take us off.

Setting sail, we next day came off a small island called Pico, to the west of Terceira, where we lay to, and one of the corvettes getting out of her station, was fired at by our ship.

CHAPTER 9

Portugal

After a fine run, we came off the coast of Portugal on the 7th of July; on Sunday the 8th we came close to shore, about fifteen miles to the north of Oporto, and sent a boat to plant a Union Jack, which we wanted to see if anyone would meddle with.

Having been left for three hours, and no one coming near it, we thought we might land.

Captain Shaw having learned that it was intended to keep us on board the fleet, to act as marines, passed the word to be ready to jump into the first boats, so that when once in, they would be obliged to let us go ashore.

The boats were lowered, and our company sprung into them, and had lots of scrambling, swearing, roaring, and laughing; and when we came to the beach, one of our chaps standing on the bow of the boat was afraid to jump, so I shoved him aside, telling him to let me pass.

I got ashore well, but just as he tried it, the boat gave a lurch, and in he went, right up to his chin, roaring out, "Och me, I'm drowned entirely;" and he spluttered mightily.

We then formed on the beach, and hearing that the enemy were advancing, ran across some fields towards a wood. Here we had the first glimpse of them, in the shape of cavalry; but the ships firing a few rounds over our heads, sent them to the right about.

We now formed on the top of a hill; near the wood, and Colonel Hodges called out, "I'll give eight dollars to whoever gets me a mule;" but none was to be found till we seized one upon which a countryman was riding up a lane.

We then marched through the wood, light company in front, and I, with two men on the look-out, in advance of the company, posted myself at a gate, placing a sentinel on each side.

I was moving about to reconnoitre, when presently one of them, Leslie, came to me and said, "There's a man in the wood."

"Why not shoot him?"

"I did not like."

"But what brought you here?"

"To tell you."

"Well, let 's see if we can find him." So with musket cocked, I accompanied him; but seeing nothing, said, "Now, take your post again, and if you see any thing, fire at it; but mind, if I see you offer to leave your post again, either to come to me or to run away, I'll put a bullet through you."

"Will you?" said he.

"Ay, that I will, you may depend on on't." Poor fellow, it was a new kind of work to him, and he was in a terrible fright all that night, turning his head in every direction, as if the devil were alongside.

Some of our young chaps were very different, and one, Witney, said he would fire at an old woman if she came in his way, "he wanted a shot so bad."

Receiving orders to advance, we arrived at a village, and took possession of a large house, and placing piquets on three cross roads, awaited the coming up of the Portuguese. During the night I had to relieve sentries, and went foraging for eatables. Getting into a convent, and hearing a noise, I kept my musket ready in case of accidents; but, listening at the door, I found it was some of our own fellows on the same errand as myself.

I was fortunate enough to pick up a loaf, and a bottle of *aguadente*, and passing through a garden, shook myself some figs off.

In the morning the Portuguese came up, and the Emperor kept us in the rear, after we had run the chance of any danger that might have met our landing. It was also a part of our duty this day to bring up all stragglers, and a pretty day's march we had of it, under a broiling sun, over brooks, hills, bridges, &c.

The next day, the 9th, we entered Oporto, without having fired a shot, and marching through the town, cheered by many of the inhabitants, formed in the arsenal square.

It was tremendously hot, and being very thirsty I said to my next man, I would have a glass of wine, as we had taken Oporto; but Captain Shaw seeing me drinking, was very angry at me for showing a bad example to the men.

We were quartered in the convent of St. Lazarus, receiving strict orders not to molest the monks, who lived in fine style; but the temptations were too much for us poor men.

Unluckily for some fine salted pigs' heads, they fell in our way, and were soon cleared, the vegetables in the garden soon disappeared also. The best of all were the pigs themselves—we had leave to kill those that made their way into the garden, but not to touch those in the wood and roads; however, as they did not seem half fond of the garden, we fell upon the plan of driving them in, then closing the gate and killing them.

The first night we caught three, which the Captain saw lying dead in the kitchen in going his rounds. The next night he saw six.

"Hello!" says he, "the pigs seem very partial to the garden; but are you sure you found them all there?"

No reply.

"Who is butcher?"

No reply.

"Oh, I see how it is, but take care I don't catch you at it."

But notwithstanding all his sharpness, we managed to keep ourselves well supplied with pork, and also contrived to get a fair share of *aguadente* in exchange for anything we could carry away from the convent.

On the 14th, at one o'clock in the morning, learning that the Miguelites were near Valongo, about three leagues off, we marched there, reaching it about half-past four, but the enemy had retreated towards Penafiel. After refreshing ourselves with bread taken from the baskets of fifty mules we met on the road to Oporto, we marched a league further, where we learned that they were as far to our right, but, in following them, we went a league round.

We numbered between 3000 and 4000, and it was thought that the Miguelites were more than double that number. Arriving at a village where we rested awhile, we were allowed an hour's foraging, and our company caught a big porker, in a farm-yard, and picked up lots of cabbages, &c.

We singed and roasted the pig all in one, and, as it was getting ready, cut off slices to our hearts' content.

I went foraging for poultry and got three, so we had a famous feast. We then went in search of wine, and saw an old Portuguese about eighty, the only person left in the village. I asked him to get us some, and he managed to fill my canteen out of somebody's cellar.

I here saw three Portuguese cavalry in a yard; they said to me, "Englishman? Englishmans love wine."

I said, "Wilt have any?"

"No, get from old man."

We then returned to Valongo, where we rested, taking possession of the houses, and at two next morning returned to Oporto, carrying with us from Valongo everything we could lay our hands on.

About three days after, marching to the left of the Valongo road, from four in the morning till about twelve o'clock, the great heat had completely knocked us up; but I, not being quite so bad as the rest, had to draw the company's rations of bread and beef.

After placing them under a hedge, I told the men to fall to.

"Too tired, Corporal, could not eat a bit."

"As you please about that, but if you don't, I'll make free with your share."

I then cut off a thumping beefsteak, and, thinking that I might have some hard work in the course of the day, cooked it nicely, with all the gravy in, to make me strong and long-winded; I might have saved myself the trouble, for we were soon after ordered to retreat. While in the village, one of our men had visited a wine-cellar, and getting drunk, was ordered to receive three dozen with a canteen belt. While tying him up, the French began to cry out that he should not be flogged. We very nearly had a bit of row, but the Colonel coming up quieted them, by explaining that as the man had got drunk when near the enemy he ought to be punished.

On our retreat, a sergeant of our company, vexed at not having had a shot at the enemy, fired at a donkey in a field near the road. The men quizzing him, he got angry and quarrelled with one of the privates. Our march was through a valley, and when ordered to halt, the sergeant was on the face of the hill. As we were resting at the bottom, the scamp suddenly cocked his piece and fired amongst us, luckily, without doing any harm. He was immediately seized, and the Colonel being told of it, ordered me and four men to take him on to Oporto. We pinioned his arms, and marched off with him, but the Caçadores, through whom we had to pass, having found out what he had been about, gave us some trouble in preventing them from ill using him.

After we had marched about a mile, he begged hard that I would loosen the strap round his arms.

"I should not much mind," I said; "but you might try to bolt, and as I should catch you with a leaden messenger, if I killed or winged you, they might ask me what business I had to let you loose; so, safe bind safe find."

Again, coming into town, he wanted to blarney me over to let him walk free with us, and when I told him just to take it easy, he began to vow vengeance against me. I did not mind that, and lodged him in the guard house. He never was tried, but was shipped off to England soon after.

CHAPTER 10

Fighting the 'Migs'

On the 17th July, hearing that the Miguelites were strong on our left, we marched out on the Valongo road (being about 250 British, the same number of French, and 400 Portuguese), expecting to be back that night or the next morning. About six o'clock we halted on the ground the Migs had been on the night before, and then marching, followed the guerrillas till we reached Penafiel, about thirty miles from Oporto.

Here the enemy made a regular stand, but after a good deal of musket work, and bringing our two small guns to bear upon them, they gave way, and we took possession of the hill on which the town is placed.

The day was most dreadfully hot, and having had no food for nearly forty-eight hours, and a long march, climbing hills and hard fighting, all of us were half dead with fatigue, and sixteen actually died; but as, during the march, the men were constantly leaving the ranks to break into houses for food and wine, orders were given to cut down anyone who should do so, and on Lieutenant Boulger declaring he could not, he was told he would be put under arrest.

I had almost gone off the same way myself, as, when I was getting over a low wall, I felt so weak that I could not manage it, and lay for some time with my head on one side and my feet on the other. The officers were no better off; Captains Staunton and Shaw were thought to be dead, but after some time recovered. The Portuguese fired into the town, and burned a convent, which we all plundered, and got lots of good things of all kinds, from whiskey to champagne, and London porter, left behind by the friars, many of whom we saw with the guerrillas, and several of whom were killed in the action.

We remained here till ten o'clock on the morning of the 19th, when a large body of Miguelites coming upon us, obliged us to retreat in double quick time to Oporto.

For my part I was so knocked up, that I was obliged to throw my firelock, belt, and pouch, into a bullock cart, and staggered along like a drunken man, but kept up as I could.

We formed on a rising ground near Oporto, but the Migs thought it unsafe to come nearer, so we got back to the town, more dead than alive.

Three days after this (22nd) we advanced to Valongo. Our company lay on the left of the road, at the top of the town, as a reserve. The enemy came down in thousands upon the 10th and 15th Caçadores, who, not knowing of our being posted here, retired before their charge.

Colonel Hodges cried out, "Lie still, men, and don't show the red coats till I give you the word."

We were not above 400, all hiding behind a wall, and when the enemy had got to within twenty yards of us, Colonel Hodges called out, "Spring up and give them a volley;" this we did in famous style, and set them scampering off. The grenadier company was now sent to drive them in the rear, and, with the help of the Caçadores who had again advanced, we took a number of prisoners, and ammunition, cars, &c. We now hobbled back to Oporto, very tired; our wounded crawling along, some limping, and others with both arms in slings.

We bivouacked in the wood and round the town, and next day, 23rd, advanced to Ponte Ferreira, about nine miles off. Marching between two hills, we saw the Miguelites in possession of the bridge on the opposite side of the river.

We advanced, and our Captain jumped in, his frock-coat floating on the surface; we all followed, and finding that my cartouche-box was likely to get wet, I pulled it round to the front under my chin, and held up my firelock, the water being breast high. The Caçadores and ourselves now made a desperate attack on the enemy, driving them off the hill into the wood, from which they would not come out, thinking they had got a safe berth; but our company, after losing two men, one a volunteer officer, hunted them out.

Just at the entrance of the wood a shot came from a tree, and wounded a Frenchman close to me; he looked up, swore a French oath, cocked his firelock, held her up, and in a moment there was a crashing of the branches, and a great big fellow came tumbling at our feet. The fool should have kept himself quiet, and no harm would have happened to him.

While the others were charging up the hill, the light company, keeping at the bottom, attacked those in the wood, Captain Shaw calling, "Come on, my lads, let's drive them out and keep them going:" and having accomplished this, with a part of the company took the hill in another direction, leaving twelve of us and fifteen Frenchmen to follow the Migs we had driven through the wood.

While chasing them, one fellow kept running just before me, and having a musket in his hand, although I might probably have got before him and have taken him prisoner, yet,

being afraid of getting shot myself, and it being impossible to halt, I held out at him and shot him through the back.

We were now to the right of the rest of the company. I got under a rock on the top of a hill, down which we had driven the Migs, and on seeing a troop of cavalry coming up to attack us, said to Lieutenant Burton, "Do you see what is coming, sir; we haven't sufficient men to form square—we must retreat best way we can towards the wood."

This we did in double quick time. Having my haversack slung in front, it hindered me retreating, so I took out my knife, and cutting the straps, left it for the Miguelites.

A Frenchman, incommoded by his great coat, being horse-collar fashion round his neck, asked me, in running, to pull it off. I tried to do so, but in tugging at it he came to the ground, and I fear the poor fellow had bad luck. Our cartridges being too large mine was only half way down, so I was forced to carry the ramrod in my hand, and the cavalry being within thirty yards of us, I threw myself, ramrod, gun, and all, over a wall among some thorns, which nearly tore my eyes out. The cavalry charged up to the wall, were too late for me, but cut through the shako of Corporal Burns, without touching his head.

As soon as I found myself on the right side of the wall, says I to myself, "Fair play's a jewel;" so driving the charge home, held out at my friend the cavalry man who had made the slash at me, and made him and the ground acquainted. We were again compelled to retreat, but a reinforcement of Caçadores having come up, Colonel Hodges, who was galloping about, waving his sword and cheering us, called out, "Now, men, cross the river, and drive the ruffians back once more."

Captain Shaw called, "My company, I know you'll follow me."

"Captain Shaw, we'll follow you wherever you lead us," was our answer.

We did manage to cross, but were again driven back.

We tried it once more, but with the same success; and Captain Shaw, who was standing on the bank, said to me, "Corporal Knight, don't come further, you'll just have to go back again."

I said, "Captain, you have been through three times, and I'll be through three times also." He laughed.

We were at last successful, and charged up a lane in which they had placed a gun, but which, all the better for us, they fired by mistake on their own men; and thinking, from the way we pressed on, that we were the devil's own, they set off, leaving us masters of the field.

So we got all the glory of the day, but nothing more; for it was near night, and we were mighty hungry, and had no rations to stop the hunger.

A soldier must not be too nice, so I cut off the hind quarter of one of the cavalry horses, that had bothered us so much, and putting a lump on the end of my ramrod, roasted it at the fire, and deuced good it tasted. The officers were worse cut up than the men, and were very thankful to get a bit of horseflesh.

The Quartermaster Sergeant said, "Who has any water? the Colonel wants some."

I had filled my canteen in crossing the river the last time, and singing out, "I have some," he said:

"Give me a little; or perhaps you can spare it all."

"Let me have a mouthful, and you may keep the rest," said I.

I slept soundly, breakfasting off the horse.

As we were moving off, we met two bullock-carts with provisions and wine for the English; and I got an extra share for having given up the water to the Quartermaster Sergeant.

Colonel Hodges now asked us if we were able to fight today again; to which we answered, "Yes, Colonel, whenever you like."

However, we passed over the ground they had occupied during the night, crossing the bridge they had left, and came into Oporto.

The men had received no pay for some time, and having been led to believe that it had been given out, but was withheld, most of the light company, while at St. Lazarus, marched up to the Colonel's quarters to ask him about it; and upon his assuring us that he had received none but would do his utmost to procure it in a day or two, myself and a few others were satisfied, but the greater part went straight to the Emperor to complain, and to demand their arrears.

Captain Shaw coming down to parade, and seeing only six non-commissioned officers and six privates, said, "Hello! Where's my company?"

The sergeant answered that he supposed they were gone to the Emperor.

Shortly afterwards they returned, and Colonel Hodges coming up, and seeing the men all standing about, said, "Why, what is the matter?" and on the Captain telling him, called out, "Fall in this moment." He then placed the six men who had not accompanied them as sentries, to prevent their getting out, and ordered the non-commissioned officers to retire, the parade being over.

I went to my room, took off my accoutrements, and then went out to have a chat and a bit of fun with the market girls. While with them a corporal came and said, "Knight, the Colonel wants you."

"What may that be for?" says I.

"He has been told that you were one of the mutineers."

"Oh, indeed, and if I was one of them, how could I be on parade?"

"He has been told that you ran away and left them."

"Well, I suppose I must go."

On getting to the room I found him giving them it in proper style. Captain Shaw observing me, said, "Corporal Knight, I hear that you were the ringleader in this business, and you are the last man I would have suspected to be guilty of such un-soldier-like conduct."

"Sir, he is a liar whoever told you so."

Colonel Hodges hearing us speak, turned round, and, shaking his fist at me, said, "I'll give you 300 for this. I made you a Corporal because I thought you deserved it; but I'll cut off your stripes and work you for it."

"As you please, sir; but I suppose that a man will be allowed to say something for himself."

"To be sure; but what can you say?"

"Only, sir, that whoever told you that I had any hand in this mutiny, told you a lie, and I should like to see the man face to face that charged me with it."

"Come here," he said; and going up the rank, seized a fellow by the collar, and lugging him out, "Now, repeat your charge."

"Oh, Lord! Sir, it wasn't Corporal Knight I meant, it was another man."

"Why how dared you attempt to hurt a man's character in this manner? You scoundrel!"

So I was once more all right; but the Colonel took the wings from our company, and we did not get them again till after the fight of the 16th of September.

CHAPTER 11
The Piquet

We were now posted at the chapel of Bom Fim, guarding the lines and batteries on the Valongo and San Cosmo road; and from the headquarters of the Miguelites being on the other side of the hill Lugar das Antas, which both were very anxious to hold, many a hard tussle, and many a hard day and night's work we had here.

A short time before the affair of the 16th September, being on piquet duty on a hill near Bom Fim, on a very wet night, Lieutenant Vanzeller led the men to some huts on the left for shelter. Before lying down he borrowed my knapsack for a pillow, saying, "Corporal, keep a sharp look-out on the sentries," of whom there were seven; we had four during the day and seven at night.

Putting my musket under my arm, and with my great coat on, I walked about, well soaked with rain. Every four hours I had to relieve the sentries, and in doing so we had to cross a field near the enemy's piquet, and were sure to be saluted with a volley.

This night-work used to vex me terribly, for the sight of one of my eyes being bad, and the other not quite right, I used to be tumbling into holes and over trees, and losing my way. But though my night thoughts were of a very dull kind, and often led me to think myself a fool for coming out, daylight always brought me round.

Early next morning Captain Shaw came to us with an officer (Lieutenant Jenkins) and fifteen men, and telling us that he was going to cut off a troop of cavalry (the officer belonging to which every morning used, in defiance, to wave his sword with his cap on it round his head), said he wanted six volunteers. I immediately stepped out, being always willing to follow my Captain, and five others joining us, we all advanced to where two roads met, and halted.

Captain Shaw then took six men and went round about half a mile, to force the dragoons up a lane, so narrow that, if once there, they must have surrendered to us, who would have had them in front and rear.

Standing under a wall at a corner of the lane, up which we expected the enemy to ride, I heard voices overhead, and looking up saw a girl, who was leaning over the wall; she handed me a bunch of grapes, and, while eating them, I heard the report of a carbine; we immediately stood to our arms, expecting to see the cavalry driven up by the Captain, but were grievously disappointed on seeing him and his party returning alone.

It seemed, that in passing under the rock on which the dragoon sentry was placed, they had been observed by him, and he immediately firing his piece, the troop (forty-three men) had mounted and rode to the rear. The Captain was vexed at losing them, for he had planned it so well, that a minute more or less would have put them all in our hands.

Four or five days after this, expecting to be attacked, we placed additional sentries in order to prevent the enemy getting round us. In the morning, the officer of the piquet (Lieutenant Walsh) having brought his men from the top of the hill, Captain Shaw came up to learn the reason, and on

Lieutenant Walsh saying, that it was to keep the body of the piquet out of sight, the Captain ordered him immediately to return to the top, his proper post.

Two men had been placed on a wall, from which there was a good look-out. One of them was a great big fellow, whom Captain Shaw used to call "the big coward;" and so he proved at this time, for he and the other man deserted their posts.; but the Captain observing this, asked me the reason.

"Don't know, sir; I've just been at the other sentries; but I'll see."

Finding no one at the place, and knowing whom I had stuck there, I guessed that I'd find them anywhere but in front; and sure enough I caught them in a hole at the back of the hill, and lugging them out, told them I had half a mind to shoot them. I forced them back to their posts, and frightened them into staying there, by swearing that I would put a bullet through them if I found them away from it again; and if I had done so they would, have richly deserved it, as their cowardice might have ruined the whole affair, and have cost us our lives.

Although there was much firing between the piquets on our left, we were not engaged, and when we heard it cease were marched back to the barracks.

At night we were again led out, and about eleven o'clock a body of 400 or 500 of the enemy came down, and gave us several salvos; but not knowing our true position, their shots were directed obliquely and did little damage. As we were lying down waiting their approach, Captain Shaw called:

"Take care, men, that if you are forced to fall back, you do not tumble into the quarry in the wood."

However, the enemy did not think proper to attempt this, so we marched quietly back to our barracks.

Until the 16th of September we had a good deal of work in keeping up our piquets, which led to frequent skirmishes; and if anything serious was attempted it was always sure to be on a Sunday, which made us say among ourselves of that day, "praying in the morning, and fighting in the evening."

CHAPTER 12
Attack of 16th September

On the 15th of September, Captain Mitchell gave me a Cruzado Nova, and ordered me to take two invalids to the hospital in the town.

Colonel Burrell and his men had just arrived, and two of them getting hold of me we drank so much *aguadente*, that both of us became so very tipsy that we were picked up by the police and put into the guard-house.

One of my companions was robbed by one of the Portuguese, and telling me of it, I first blackguarded the thief, and then knocked him down, and the other fellow seeing this, ran away and left me; but the officer of police forgave me, and so did Captain Shaw when I went to the barracks.

The next morning, as I was sleeping off the drink in the guard-room, I heard shots, and, jumping up, asked for my accoutrements.

"Corporal Knight, you were drunk last night, and the sergeant sent them to the store-room."

"Curse the sergeant," said I, and rushed to the store, picked up belt, not cleaned for a month—all the same in a fight—perhaps never might come back to pipe-clay it, and lined firelock and bayonet, forgetting to try if they fitted.

I found Major Shaw on the Lugar das Antas, with about eighty men, keeping back a body of about 1500, who expected to see the few English take to their heels as soon as they showed themselves on the brow of the hill; but they found they had met with customers not to be easily frightened, and who, knowing every yard of the ground, could do a deal of mischief, without much exposing themselves.

However, we were gradually getting driven in, when Major Staunton, with the Grenadiers, and a company of Caçadores, advanced to Major Shaw's assistance, and charged the Miguelites with such fury that they could not stand it; but he himself, to the great distress of all of us, was mortally wounded in the charge. On joining my company in the fight, my firelock flashed twice, and, mad as the devil, I smashed her in two on the ground.

Seeing a young fellow wounded in the thigh, and hopping along with the blood streaming down, I said to him:

"You have no more use for your firelock, come, give her to me like a good fellow."

But he would not; so advancing for twenty yards without one, and seeing three of the enemy lying dead, I took one of theirs and primed it, but it likewise flashing.

"Blest," says I, "if I am going to have a rap at them to-day. Dick, lend me your worm."

I then laid down behind some stones, having no fancy to be shot while drawing the charge of a gun. On getting out the charge I primed and loaded again, and she smacked off beautifully, and never again failed me the whole day.

The enemy were rallied by their officers, but we hallooed, and driving them back, tried to get before them to make prisoners; but they were too nimble, and got into a wood, and it being now night all our men retired, with the exception of Sergeant Willougby, John Germain, and myself.

We kept firing at them for some time by the flashes of their guns; and a big yellow house on the hill, and some others, having been set on fire, and past which we had to run, they saw us plainly, and sent a lot of bullets whizzing past us, but made nothing of it.

A few days after this, wanting to get some money from my Captain (now Captain Mitchell), I found him and Captain Chinnock in his quarters opposite the barracks. The latter asked me what I wanted.

"Some money, sir."

"Do you understand, 'Right about three-quarters face.'"

"Yes, sir, very well."

"Let's see it.... Now then, 'Quick march.'"

I stepped out, and coming to the door, was expecting the "Halt," but he let me pass outside, and, laughing, said:

"Now you are on the right side to be off."

I was vexed at being done in this way by one not my own officer, and replied:

"Sir, you asked me just now to show you 'Right about three-quarters face;' I'll now show you, if you please, 'Left about three-quarters face;'" and wheeling round, and giving myself the word, marched into the house again. They both laughed at my doubling on them so, and Captain Mitchell gave me my money.

He then said, "Do you understand cooking?"

"Yes, sir."

"Well, there is a piece of beef, which we wish baked with some potatoes."

I immediately set about it, but having too many potatoes in the dish, the meat was done dry before they were ready. They ordered all to be dished up, and beginning to the potatoes, they found them hard, and began to blow me up, and quiz me about being a bad cook.

"The potatoes are hard, sure enough," said I, "but better that way than none; but you didn't give me time enough."

"Well, well," said they, "up with the lot; shoulder the pot and march."

Getting leave to go into Oporto one afternoon, I unfortunately got tipsy, and, measuring my length on the ground, fell asleep. On awaking in the morning the devil might have danced a hornpipe in my pockets, and the silver buckle of my Order of the Tower and Sword had gone with my money.

I attended parade, and returning to Oporto, was puzzling my head how to raise the wind for a new buckle. Thinks I: *all's fair in war; the scamps cleaned me out, and I may as well do the same to them.* So posting off to the quay, to my great joy, discovered one of our fellows lying dead drunk. My fingers were soon in his pockets, and found enough to get me what I wanted.

Next morning I met the very chap in the street, and coming up to me, he said

"Corporal, I wish you would lend me your knife, to take a splinter out of my finger."

"Is it sore?" said I.

"Yes, very; but there is something sorer."

"What is that?"

"Why, the fact is, I got drunk in the town last night, and when I was asleep some thieving blackguard came and stole my money."

"What scamps there are here," said I; "it was only the night before that one of them robbed me in the same way."

"Well," said he, "let's keep a sharp look-out, and if I get a hold of the scoundrel that tricked me, I'll make his bones sore for a month."

Thinks I to myself, *many thanks for your kind wishes*; but pitying the poor devil, with his long face, I took him into a wine-shop, and treated him (with his own money) to a bottle of wine.

Being one day on duty, to examine all who should pass the lines, a man came along with two large bundles on his shoulder, and not liking his appearance, and seeing the sentry feel his pockets very carelessly, I searched them myself, and finding bullets in his waistcoat pocket, ordered him to open his packs. This he did very unwillingly, and we found in them—shirts, &c., two bottles of spirits, and letters for the enemy.

On seeing this I sent for the Captain of the post, a Portuguese, who could speak both languages, and he ordered the man and his bundles off to prison in town. On hearing this my gentleman became abusive; but the Captain, drawing his sword, belaboured him so, that he was glad to get away, although it were to a prison.

Chapter 13

I am Wounded

When on piquet duty on the night of the 27th, there was a most tremendous storm of rain, thunder, and lightning, and Lieutenant Vanzeller, the officer of the guard, got out of the small house made of boughs, under an oak tree, into the open field, to be safe from the lightning.

The rain fell in torrents, causing streams to flow down the hill; but one of our corporals was lying on the ground as sound asleep as if he had been in his quarters, although the water was like to have carried him away, and the thunder and lightning were such as I had never before met with.

The 28th was a good night, and I had some rest, and much need I had of it, as at break of day, on Saturday the 29th, immense masses of the Miguelites were seen approaching.

Major Shaw immediately fell us in at the barracks, hoped we would stand by him, desiring us to keep ourselves well covered by the walls and hillocks, and never to fire without being sure of our man. He also told us we were likely to require our bayonets, and put us through the charge.

Our piquets, after showing good fight, were obliged to give way before the tremendous firing upon them; but Colonel Burrell, now planting himself in our barrack-house with some men, the Major took the rest, and, lining all the walls and ditches with them, peppered and astonished the Migs in famous style.

Catching it, like most others this day, I can't describe all that took place from my own observation; but this I know, that had it not been for the most determined pluck and good management of the 211 English and 300 French, who were alive this morning, Oporto would as surely have been plundered by the Miguelites, as it is certain that it was this hope, and the number of friars with them, which made them fight so desperately. When first I heard a gun fired in the morning, I got up on the top of the barracks, from whence I could see over several miles of ground, and perceived three large columns coming on.

Soon after I cried out, "Up, men, we'll have a smart day's work."

And one, half asleep, yawned out, "What's the matter?"

"Just come to the window, and you'll see something to open your eyes."

We had no time to get rations, and I was one of the party which marched to the right of the barracks, and extended beneath a wall a quarter of a mile off. Our orders were to lie there, and not to fire till our piquets, about 200 yards in front were driven in.

This soon occurred, and the enemy thinking they had it all their own way, advanced rapidly, in a horse-shoe shape; but all of us under cover, jumping up, let fly among their heavy columns, and made them stagger.

We kept pouring it into them, but, notwithstanding our shelter, were losing many men and officers from the showers of balls rattling among us.

Captain Mitchell was standing, with myself and a sergeant, about thirty yards to the right of the company, and said to me, "Knight, this is hot work; it will be my turn soon, I dare say: but never mind, my lads, hold on."

Major Shaw was moving about from one place to another, directing and encouraging all; and, for our comfort, one of our look-outs, in a house behind, kept constantly calling out that fresh columns of the enemy were coming down upon us.

Captain Walsh fell from a shot in the shoulder, then Captain Chinnock from one in the head, and both were carried to the rear.

I had now fired off sixty-three rounds, and with smoke and the heat of the day was as black as a sweep.

After being a short time without ammunition, during which we kept throwing down stones on the heads of those attempting to climb up, twenty rounds were served out.

In order not to waste time in putting them into my pouch, I laid them down before me that they might be handy. I had fired twice; but while loading the third time, I was dropped by a wound on the thigh, and fell on the wall, with my gun across it. I fired her off the third time, and then cried, "Lads, I have had enough;" the blood was running from me fast, and I got faint.

The Migs were now advancing in great force, and I called out:

"For God's sake, carry me to the rear; I am sure I would have done the same for you."

But they answered, "We can't, we have enough to do to keep them back."

I then asked a sergeant, and he carried me twenty yards and put me down.

Our men were now retiring, and as they were leaving me behind, I cried out, "Carry me, carry me; I shall be cut to pieces;" and almost immediately the sergeant and my other comrade were knocked over.

Seeing how it was, I thought I might as well try to crawl to the rear, and managed to get along about a quarter of a mile, but the motion made the blood gush out afresh.

The bullets and balls were flying about like hailstones; but I got behind the battery at the rear of the church of Bom Fim, and immediately fell asleep.

On awaking, a Portuguese Captain told me I had better go to the hospital; but on my telling him I was not very well able, being badly wounded, he very kindly offered to send two men to assist me: this offer I refused, but accepted of a mule, on which I went.

While passing through the town, the inhabitants seemed much afraid and alarmed by the number of the wounded who were coming in. After waiting seven hours the surgeon came, and the ball being still in, he made three slashes, then probed and extracted it.

In about three weeks we were carried on stretchers by four men to our own hospital, and here I was kept till January, 1833.

Adjutant Brown was removed at the same time as myself. On starting, he told the Portuguese bearers to be careful and not to let him fall; but, in turning a corner sharply, they slipped, and fairly shot him out.

"You scoundrels," said he, "did I not tell you to be careful."

Our little battalion was terribly cut up on the 29th of September; 109 rank and file out of 211, and every officer, with the exception of Lieutenant Vanzeller, being killed or wounded. Major Shaw getting hit half a dozen times, one wound on the breast from a spent ball knocking him over, and rendering him insensible for some time. However, he recovered, leading his men throughout the day, and with the French (who were also terribly cut up), and a few Portuguese cavalry, the Miguelites were driven back; but this they did not accomplish till near seven o'clock at night, having been hard at it since six in the morning.

The wounded, owing to the great number who had suffered on the 29th, were exceedingly ill off, having neither sufficient medical attendance nor accommodation, nor in fact any thing requisite.

Mr. Alcock was our doctor, and no man could have done more than him, but he had not sufficient assistance of any kind.

We were all crammed into small places, and, owing to the bad air, dirtiness, and want of attention, only those who had good constitutions got out after having once entered.

But in saying this, I am speaking of some of the early months, for during the starvation time the hospital rations were never reduced; and that again had the effect of bringing us many skulkers, fit enough for work, but who, during the time that so many of the English officers were quarrelling and fighting among themselves, could do pretty much as they liked, and naturally preferred a good covering, with full rations, to out-of-door duty, with an ounce or two of rice and salt fish.

In fact, to such a state of disorder had they got, that in the month of February it was found necessary to dismiss many of the officers, and to attach the men to the Scotch under my old Captain, who, with his Scotchmen, having, night and day, constant work to keep his post at Lordelo, had no time or inclination for squabbling.

A month or two previous to this, one day while ill in hospital, I wrapped a rug round me for warmth, and stepped to the window to see the Caçadores pass by: Colonel Hodges happened to be passing at the time; observing me, he called up, "Knight, how are you getting on?"

"Pretty well, sir, I thank you."

"Well, get on quickly, for you are much wanted."

"I shall, sir, and am much obliged by your kind asking."

Shortly after, and just before his sailing to England, he came to see us all in hospital, and, from the privates' room, called out to me, and in I hobbled as well as I could.

He then presented me, and eight or nine others, with the written Order of the Tower and Sword, and the ribbon and buckle belonging to it, telling us, it was for our conduct at Ponte Ferreira. This I have always worn since, and with the first seven shillings I can scrape together, shall take my Waterloo medal out of pledge, and wear it above.

The Colonel then shook me by the hand, telling me he hoped yet to see me safe in England; and on coming to London, the first place I went to was the Military Club House, where I found him, and he again shook hands with me, and said to some officers beside him, that I was a "Brave Warrior," and made me a present.

CHAPTER 14

Cats and Dogs

The only time that Colonel Shaw was laid on his back from wounds, was from two he got through both legs, in December (I think); and when I used to be hobbling along with a stick, and he on crutches, we often met, and he generally said:

"Corporal, since you entered on this affair, you surely wont give it up till we have gained what we set out for."

"Oh, sir," said I, "my soldiering days are now over, and I shall never more be able to run at, or from an enemy; and I shall be much obliged to you for a character to show. I hope, that on the whole, I have been respected as a soldier." I don't give his answer to this, but I give a copy of the certificate he wrote for me.

The place was now so closely blockaded, that, though invalided, I was unable to get away, and it was but a poor place to live in.

I was attached to Major Brownson's regiment to draw rations, and little enough we received.

They were served out at four o'clock, and consisted of two ounces of *bacalhao* (salt fish), one ounce of rice, and half a pint of wine a day—on some days six ounces of bread, and at other times none; we used besides to have a small glass of spirits every morning.

We were also in a wretched state for want of clothes and bedding. I have been four months without ever changing my clothes; some of the men were without shoes, stockings, &c, but many used to sell them, their rations, and everything they could, for *aguadente*, with which they half killed themselves.

We were in such a starving state that nothing eatable was allowed to escape. The French first showed us the example, and before long there was scarcely such a thing as a dog or cat to be seen in Oporto. We used also to collect snails, and, boiling them in two waters with a little salt, they made pretty good prog.

One day I was prowling about, outside barracks, thinking how I should get a bellyful of anything, when two of the Lancers came past.

"Hello! Corporal, why so down in the mouth?"

"It would make the devil look down," said I, "to be so starved—I could eat a horse behind the saddle."

"Well," says one of them, "come along with us, we have just been cooking some mutton broth, and you shall have some."

At this time I had not ventured upon the dogs and cats; but having seen them seized for cooking, I greatly doubted it being mutton broth. On seeing it, I said:

"Is this cat or dog?"

"Did not we say it's mutton broth."

So I drank the soup, and although, from my fears of what it might be, I felt a little squeamish, yet, not having seen it cooked, over it went, and in return for it, I thanked the lancer gentlemen.

"Ye're welcome," said they; "but here is some meat left, which you can have, for we have had a good blow-out ourselves."

So I lined up a piece and looked at it.

"Don't tell me that this is mutton—it smells so strong; I'll swear it's nothing but an old tom-cat—I think you've been tricking me."

They burst out a laughing: "Poh! never mind, you have had a good bellyful, it will do you no harm."

But I fancied all day that there was a taste in my mouth, and nearly choked myself with water, trying to put it away. However, I was soon not so nice, and looked out for cats and dogs as keenly as anyone; and one day got a terrible blowing up from an old woman who saw me looking at her cat, and thought I was going to steal it—many a bad name I got from her.

It was about this time that two of the French and one of the British were taken prisoners, and hung next day on a tree within sight of our lines; the Frenchmen's blue and our red uniform being plainly visible, and putting us all, but especially the French, in a great rage: however, there they hung for some weeks before we could get at them to cut them down, and that very morning the French bayoneted forty-two Miguelites whom they took in a field, and after that little quarter was given on either side by the French or Portuguese.

CHAPTER 15

An Adventure Near Lordelo

Expecting now to get away every day, I thought I would pay a farewell visit to my old comrades at the Foz, about four miles off; but found that I was obliged to halt at Lordelo, half-way, and to finish my journey the next day. Whilst returning, an officer of the Rocket Brigade stopped me:

"Where are you going, Corporal?"

"To Oporto, sir."

"I have been trying to get men for a Rocket Brigade, and I wish you would join us."

But I excused myself by telling him I was too lame to run.

"Well, if you won't come yourself, will you get us some men?"

"Certainly, sir."

I was at this time very ill off for food and money, and though I did not like to ask for it, I hoped he would have given me a trifle when I got to Oporto, as he promised; but not a stiver did I get, and so the Rocket Brigade was never the better for me, nor I for the Rocket Brigade.

Hobbling along towards Oporto, I heard someone sing out from a ditch on the roadside—"Help, help."

Thinking it was someone drunk I looked round, and there, sure enough, was a man in the ditch, and his mule on the other side.

"Oh, Corporal," says he, "I have had a desperate fall." And so it seemed, for his nose was nearly broken off his face.

After placing him on his mule, he asked me to guide him to his quarters at Lordelo, which I did; but on reaching this he told me it was outside the place, nearer the Foz, and across a small river. By this time he had become so very drunk, that he could not tell me where to take him to, and coming close upon the enemy's lines, I retreated, and in the dark stumbled on one of our batteries, where I learned where he lived, and taking him there, he stammered out to me to call upon him in Oporto, and he would give me something; this I afterwards did, but my gentleman never made his appearance where he promised.

I was so completely done up with the weary round, that in order to get back to Lordelo by a short cut, I crept near the enemy's battery; but, being fired at, I thought it a pity to be shot without a chance of returning the compliment, and crawled along to the Scotch barracks, where I instantly fell asleep.

The next morning I returned to Oporto, and was so hungry that I had to satisfy myself with heads of Indian corn washed down with water, and in the evening drew my small allowance of salt fish and rice for rations.

In May, sixty-three invalids, French and English, were lying at the Foz, waiting for an opportunity to embark, and were quartered in a house, the roof and walls of which were riddled with shot.

Having a friend in Oporto, I used now and then to go there to sleep, and one morning returning to the Foz, found that all had got on board, and, as they were in the roads, I had to stay behind, and was now worse off than ever, my rations being struck off for not embarking.

This I thought very hard, and applying to General

Saldanha, he attached me to the Scotch, under my old Captain, now Colonel Shaw, and with them I got on famously, as, from never having been in the town, and always close to the enemy, they were obliged to be steady, and to keep up strict discipline.

The Colonel never flogged, but if any of them did get drunk (at which time they were greater devils than any men I ever met with), or otherwise misconduct themselves, he used to punish them in ways of his own—shaving their heads, blackening their noses, taking the tartan from their bonnets, and locking them up, and especially by making them ashamed of themselves. There are some men, I am sure, whom nothing but the fear of the cat will keep in order; but I think it may be, and is very often used, when different treatment would answer the purpose much better.

My pay being now long in arrears, I was anxious for a settlement; and Sir John Doyle, who was always wanting to get into favour with the men, told me not to go without it.

It would have pleased me better if someone else than him had given me hopes of getting it, for, when in hospital, I had been told that the men had again mutinied for their pay, and that Sir John had humbugged them with fine promises of what he would do for them. but I could never learn that he did more, than to get hold of a little money intended for the recruits just arrived, and to pay it over to the old hands. It was well known to them, that he wanted to get the command of the British, and to place some friends of his own in the place of our old officers; but although Pedro did appoint him, almost every one of the officers, declaring they would not serve under him, and the kind of men he had brought with him, threw up their commissions.

Thinking that he could get the better of them, he placed

the commander, Major Shaw, under arrest, declaring he would have him tried for mutiny before the enemy, and shot! The Major, however, having his own opinion of Sir John Milley Doyle and his companions, entreated, as a particular favour, when his sword was sent for, that, as he valued it as his honour, and had had it for twenty years, it might not be touched by any of them. The same evening the Emperor, seeing how it was, reinstated the old officers, sending Major Shaw his sword back with a fine message; and from that day to this Sir John Milley Doyle has afforded much amusement to Don Pedro and others, by whistling and singing. All this made a great talk at the time.

The Miguelites had now got General Bourmont and a great parcel of French officers to lead them, and having collected all their forces close to our position, the key to the town from the river, and consequently what the enemy were most anxious to get a hold of, and for which they tried, on the 25th July, most determinedly.

I was in the heat of some of the fight, but, from my lameness, not being able to run from one place to another, I can only describe a part of it.

While at breakfast we heard the piquets engaged, and starting up, saw immense masses driving them in, and carrying fascines and ladders before them, and at the same time all the enemy's batteries poured round shot in among us.

We were driven from our barracks, and were retreating up a lane, when Colonel Shaw, who had been placing and leading other parties on the Foz road, came galloping up on his mule—"What are you at, men? Right about face—charge."

We wheeled round, and drove them again through the barracks and out of the garden, our bagpipes screeching notes of defiance all the time. A musket-ball, passing though my foraging-cap, had nearly settled me; but not being able to follow, I remained in rear, and while standing and taking a shot when I thought it might do good, Baron Cabe, the barrack-master of Oporto, came up to me, and asked if I had seen General Saldanha.

"Yes, sir, a quarter of an hour ago, passing towards the Foz."

The Baron was on a red pony, and I was leaning on one of the barrels filled with earth to shelter us, when a round shot, smashing the one next us, covered us both with earth. "Corporal, close work that," said the Baron, and rode away.

I cried out, "Sir, you had better not go further that way, or you will get into the worst of it."

"But I wish to see General Saldanha."

I think the Miguelites never fought so well as they did this day, and it was just touch and go, that they did not get the better of us. The fight continued, at regular hand to hand work, till the evening, when the Migs and their bragging Frenchmen had to retire, having lost many men, as we ourselves also did, and among others Colonel Cotter and his nephew.

My old Captain, for a wonder, got through it all without more than a scratch on the cheek; and a queer figure he was for a commanding officer, with his shaggy red whiskers and beard, his blue jacket, red cloth cap with blue tassel, and long pole in his hand—his usual dress when here.

The same night I went back to Oporto, and returned the next day to Lordelo, to have a look at the fields and places where they had been fighting.

It was clear there had been a regular set to, and that the grape and big guns had been in full play, judging from the immense number of killed of our own side, but especially of the Miguelites.

In some places great lots of them were lying huddled together, and one great fat fellow, with legs as thick as a man's body, I saw standing jammed up by a round shot between a wall and a tree. Some were terribly smashed by bars of iron two feet long, which we had let off among their heavy columns.

Having already suffered much from the stench of the bodies of those killed in former attacks, which it was dangerous to burn or bury, as the enemy always fired on our men when we attempted it, the Colonel, thinking that in this hot weather the smell of those killed the day before would cause a plague, resolved to try to get them buried.

It was ticklish work; but jumping over the wall, and holding his hands above his head, he went near one of their piquets, and an officer approaching, saluted him, and, after a little, it was agreed that each should bury or burn his own dead, and that only man for man, unarmed, should be allowed to meet to do so.

The Colonel, at the same time, gave his word that he would not allow a single man of the Miguelites to remain with him then, and refused to receive many who wished to stay; but told them, that after returning to their lines, they might come over if they liked, and some did; but whatever the reason may be, it must be allowed that the Miguelites kept exceedingly steady to their colours, and that if they deserted to us, not a few of our Portuguese, and also some British, deserted to them. At this time we had just learned that Admiral Napier had captured their fleet, and that Lisbon was ours, which we took care to spread among the Migs, supposing that they would now give over resisting us.

This, however, we have since found they had no intention of doing; but about the 10th or 12th of August, they slipped quietly away one dark night, with old Bourmont still at their head, marching for Lisbon.

Next morning I went to see their deserted batteries, and thought to myself, it was lucky the enemy had been obliged to leave them, as they were of such strength as I had not before any notion of.

CHAPTER 16

The Miguelites and Oporto

Without being a boaster, I may say that, during the whole time I was here, I don't think all the foreign troops exceeded 1000 effective men; but with the exception of one or two famous Caçadore regiments, we had no other troops to be depended upon in real hard work.

The other Portuguese regiments were well enough in their way, but could not be relied upon if good troops were opposed to them.

Often have I thought, as I do still, that 3000 of our own army, well led, would have forced the lines, and have taken Oporto any day they chose; and if the Miguelites, in their attacks on the 16th and 29th September, 4th March, and 25th July, had kept up the determination they began with, and had not been afraid of bayonet work, their immense numbers, against the handful of British, must have driven them back, or, what was more likely, have knocked every one of them over; and after that I would not have given much for Oporto, or all in it.

The Miguelites at Villa Nova used to keep playing upon the town, and a number of the inhabitants were killed; but the houses themselves, from being all built of freestone, were wonderfully little hurt.

After some time, even the women and children became

so accustomed to the shells, &c. coming among them, that on seeing one alight, they would throw themselves on the ground, and, lying down, patiently await its explosion.

The streets themselves were in a pretty state, having been broken up in all directions, and piles of stones erected across them, not less than ten feet high, and on all the roads leading to the town, stakes and lopped trees were driven into the earth to keep the Migs out.

And now, having been in Oporto since the 9th of July, 1832, about fifteen months, and during that period having undergone much suffering, and much hardship of various kinds, I left it.

On entering the town it was surrounded by fine trees, by gentlemen's seats, and by every mark of a rich, thriving place; and I left it with almost all the trees and gardens about it cut down, the houses in the neighbourhood burned and destroyed, and everything bearing the marks of devastation and destruction.

On the 10th of October I embarked on board the *Samuel* schooner, laden with wine, for Bristol, and on coming out of the river, overheard the Captain say:

"Mate, as our two passengers will be sick, they won't cost us much for prog."

I immediately said, "Oh, don't be too sure of that, and see that I don't astonish your pork barrel."

Meeting with a heavy gale in the bay of Biscay, we sprung a leak, and our two best men being on the sick list, the Captain said:

"Corporal, will you work?"

"I don't mind if I do, to save the ship."

"Well, that's right, and here are a pair of trousers and a jacket for you, don't work in these clothes."

The sea washing over the deck, we were set to the pumps,

and at first finding it very easy, I sung out, "No very hard labour this, Captain."

"Wait a little," said he; and immediately afterwards an immense wave coming over us, obliged me to hold on like grim death; but the Captain, laughing, observed, "Oh, that is only a drop, Corporal."

"I'm not afraid," said I; and getting a glass of grog, the Captain told me he would give me a glass for every hour I worked.

This was a temptation, so I kept at it for seven hours, but at last had to tell the Captain my arms could stand it no longer.

"No wonder," said he, "for you have had a devil of a spell."

My comrade was a regular lubber, skulking under the hatches, and I don't think would have stirred to help us, if it had been to save all our lives.

We were now divided into two watches, the Captain putting me in his, and promising to do something for me on landing.

Putting him in mind of what he had said to the mate on sailing, he answered, "Yes, you have cheated us about grub, but you have given us good work for it."

After meeting with some very heavy squalls, we reached Bristol, and, with the exception of something I got for my sailoring, landed without a single thing in the world but my two-year-old marine jacket, an old pair of blue trousers, and shoes, and other things much the worse for the wear.

I calculate that Don Pedro owes me £43; but although I have shown his people here all my certificates, and have been recommended to them by gentlemen in London, they tell me they can give me nothing till the whole affair is finished: but I am now too old a soldier to trust to such promises, so, as I am now pretty strong again, I must just look out for something to do, by which I may earn an honest livelihood.

Appendix

ORDER OF TOWER AND SWORD

(COPY)

*Tendo o Duque de Bragança, Regente em Nome da Rainha,
e como Gran' Mestre da Antiga e Muito-nobre ordern da Torre-e-
Espada do Valor, Lealdade e Mérito, feito enercè de nomear Cava-
lleiros da mesma Ordern a Nove Officiaes inferiores e Soldados do
Balathào de Marinha, por Decreto do primeiro de Agosto do anno
corrente, em attencáo aos extremados feitos de valor practicados no
memoravel dia vinte e tres de Julho ⋆ ⋆ ⋆ na batalha de Ponte-Fe-
rreira, assim como ⋆ ⋆ ⋆ ⋆ ennobreceram o reconliecimento do dia
anterior: E sendo-lhe presente que fora um dos que bem mereceram
aquella distinccáo o Soldado do mesmo Corpo Knight.*

*Ha por bem couceder-lhe faculdade para poder usar livremente
da respectiva insignia, sem embargo ⋆ ⋆ ⋆ faltarem ainda as forma-
lidades prescriptas pelo Alvard de vinte ⋆⋆⋆⋆ Julho de mil oito
centos trinta e ⋆ ⋆ ⋆ ⋆ ⋆ ⋆ ⋆ ⋆⋆ ⋆ ⋆ ⋆ ⋆ sentar na Chancellcia
da Ordern.*

Paço ña Porto em 19 de Outubro de 1832.

(Signed) *Marquess de Palmella*

(The stars denote that the original is illegible at that part.)

Oporto
4th December, 1832
I certify that Corporal Knight was under my command
while I was Captain of the Light Company, when he always
conducted himself like a good soldier. Since I have commanded the battalion, I have had many opportunities of
seeing his conduct in action, and, without disparagement to
any, I have never seen a braver soldier, or one more anxious
to do his duty at all times and under all circumstances.

(Signed) *Charles Shaw*
Major, British Battalion

The bearer, Corporal Thomas Knight, I have known for
twelve months; he was in the Company under my command, and has been with me in several actions. His conduct
has always been that of a good soldier. He leaves this service
in consequence of a severe wound which he received on
the 29th September, 1832.

(Signed) *Bruce Mitchell*
Captain, commanding Light Company
British Battalion
December 4, 1832
Oporto

I certify that Thos. Knight is rendered incapable of service, by a wound through the groin, received in the action
of the 29th of September.

(Signed) *Rutherford Alcock*
Acting Staff Surgeon
Monday, January 7, 1833

(Copy)

By order of General Stubbs, Mr. Harper will immediately settle the accounts of the bearer, Thomas Knight, late of the 2nd regiment of English Marines.

(Signed) *J. J. Loureiro*
Chief of the Staff
Oporto
12th April, 1833

It is impossible for me to settle the account of Thomas Knight, until a general statement of the men's accounts takes place with Mr. Sandford, the Commissary General of the squadron.

(Signed) *J. Harper*

(Copy)

The bearer, Thomas Knight, served as Corporal under my command, in the service of H. M. F. Majesty, the Queen of Portugal; he always conducted himself as a gallant and good soldier, both in the field and in quarters.

He was severely wounded on the 29th September, 1832, before Oporto, and is well deserving of any recompense that the Portuguese authorities in this country may think proper to afford him.

(Signed) *G. Lloyd Hodges*
London
16th November, 1833

(Copy)

The bearer, Corporal Thomas Knight, was attached to the 2nd British regiment, under my command at Oporto, for the purpose of being rationed until an opportunity offered of giving him a passage to England, in consequence of the severe wounds he received before Oporto, on the 29th September, 1832, which obliged him to be invalided. That Corporal Knight well deserves (from his gallant conduct) any recompense Her Most Faithful Majesty's authorities in this country may think proper to afford him.

(Signed) *William Henry Brownson*
Late Major, commanding
2nd British Regiment at Oporto
London
19th November, 1833

(COPY)

From the character of the officers who have signed the above certificates, and from my own recollections of the individual therein mentioned, I consider him strongly entitled to the consideration of Her Most Faithful Majesty's Government, for his well-earned claims.

(Signed) *G. R. Sartorius*
Vice-Admiral
Portuguese Service
December 12, 1833

Henry Curling's*
Anecdotes

---

* Henry Curling was the 'writer for hire' responsible for penning the famous memoir of Rifleman Harris.

Rifleman Harris

"I remember," said an old 95th man,[*] "whilst in Spain, hearing how lightly the French had esteemed us, before finding out what sort of stuff we were made of. Some of the prisoners we had taken, communicated to our men that General Junot, when he heard that the English were in Portugal, had made a speech, and told his army that they would quickly teach the English a lesson. 'When we get at them,' he said, 'we will drive them into the sea in a very short time.'"

---

[*] Benjamin Harris, 95th Regiment.

General Crawford
by Rifleman Harris[*]

General Crawford was a stern man, but then he was a real soldier. I never saw his fellow for daring, and that all knew both above and below him. I think I knew as much of him as any man in the Rifles, for he oft-times held a few minutes conversation with me when on the march. He was pleased to hold me in his favour because, being a shoemaker, and constantly at work when the fight or march was over, he said I was an industrious and useful man. Crawford, indeed, seldom failed to praise a man when he distinguished himself in any way.

Private O'Hara came under the notice of Crawford at Buenos Ayres. O'Hara was in the 54th Regiment. He saved the General's life, for a Spaniard having, unseen by Crawford, got close to him, levelled his firelock, and was just about to pull the trigger when O'Hara rushed upon and killed him.

Crawford was so much pleased with this act of O'Hara's, that he persuaded him to join the Rifles, where he greatly distinguished himself, and became a favourite with the whole corps.

---

[*] Benjamin Harris, 95th Regiment, as told to Henry Curling.

During the retreat to Corunna, he also distinguished himself greatly. In short, a more hardy, resolute Irish soldier I never beheld. When the Rifles went to Spain the second time, O'Hara was with them, and, for some time, behaved as usual; but, to the astonishment of officers and men, he one day, without any apparent cause, deserted to the French. Every man in the regiment felt dreadfully put out, but Crawford was furious. He vowed that, if he could ever get near O'Hara, he would either take or slay him with his own hands.

At the siege of Rodrigo, Crawford saw O'Hara. He caught sight of him whilst fighting in the very midst of the *mêlée,* and jumping from his horse, sprang among the enemy, and grasped him by the belt. But it seemed as if O'Hara, who feared no other living man, feared his old commanding officer, for he fled from him with such alacrity, that he tore his belt, and escaped.

Many of the Rifles saw the transaction, and told it to their comrades; and Crawford himself was heard to describe how nearly he had got O'Hara.

"Damn him," he said, "if I could have caught him I would have killed him."

Crawford was himself killed, I think, the day afterwards.

Anecdote of
Ciudad Rodrigo

After the siege of Rodrigo, several Englishmen who deserted to the French, and were re-taken, were tried by court-martial, and ordered to be shot. They were all good specimens of the dare devils of the war, and bore their sentence with the greatest nonchalance.

"Take my shoes," one of them said to a soldier near, "they are better than yours, and you will want them."

Whilst standing before a pit, which had been dug for them, and whilst the firing party were drawn up, ready to give the fatal volley, another of the culprits, on looking down, and observing the hole half full of water, remarked to the man next to him:

"You see they are going to give us a watery grave."

When the volley was fired, all fell but one man, who remained standing, apparently untouched.

Some of the soldiers, horrified at the sight, were in hopes the unhappy culprit would have been permitted to live. But the indignation of the firing party against culprits, who had committed the heinous crime of fighting against them in the ranks of the enemy, was so great, that they did not give him a chance.

Reloading in haste, several men ran up to the poor fellow, and blew his brains out.

"He thought he was going to escape," observed one of the firing-party, as they leisurely returned to the ranks, "but he was mistaken."

Picton at Waterloo

I once heard an anecdote of Picton, from an officer, who was himself at Waterloo.

Picton, I was told by this officer, was wounded the day before Waterloo, but had concealed his hurt, and with the most heroic fortitude remained in the field.

During the night, however, the agony of his wound obliged him to send for a surgeon, who remained with him until dawn; and, on his leaving, Picton thus addressed him:

"You say that my wound is dangerous—mortal; that I am unfit for duty, and must be represented so to the Duke?"

"Such is my opinion," said the medical man. "I think it would be impossible for you to take command of your division."

"Leave me to judge of that, Sir," said Picton, "and in the meanwhile, allow me to ask you a question. From your long knowledge of me, do you consider me capable of strictly keeping my word?"

"I have every cause to believe so," returned the surgeon, "but why the question, Sir Thomas?"

"Simply for this reason," returned Picton, "that I have made up my mind to be in the field with my brigade; and I give you my word of honour, both as a gentleman and a soldier, that if you place my name in your report as unfit for duty, I will shoot you with my own hand."

The surgeon shrugged his shoulders, shook Picton by the hand, and withdrew.

The gallant General's name was accordingly omitted amongst the wounded; and, as his wish had often been expressed, that he might die amidst the blaze of battle, he was gratified.

The Duke at Waterloo

Whilst the Duke was cantering along the field, just before the battle began, and looking precisely as he might often have been observed when taking his ride through Hyde Park, he suddenly pulled up, put his glass to his eye, and remained looking intently at a group of mounted officers on the enemy's side.

They were Napoleon and his staff.

Whilst the Duke was observing them with some little curiosity, an aide-de-camp, seeing they were within cannon range, suggested that some balls might immediately be sent amongst them.

The Duke took his glass from his eye in a moment, glanced indignantly at the officer, and peremptorily forbade any such measure. Clapping spurs to his horse, he pursued his career; and, with a cheerful smile, whilst his eye was everywhere, he conversed occasionally upon matters of moment, despatched his messengers, and made his arrangements, as any other man would have done at a review.

Nothing, perhaps, in any age, could compare with the coolness, nonchalance, and at the same time consummate skill and wisdom with which the Duke moved the springs of the battle. There was, I have heard, not the slightest trace of excitement to be observed in his countenance or actions during the day. Minutes seemed years to men whilst the amazing pounding and wholesale slaughter was going on; but the Duke went and came, ordered matters and repaired disasters, as if at a sham fight or a review.

The Scotch Greys

That men counted the minutes of their lives while exposed to such slaughter as they saw around them, is evident from the following anecdote, which I had from the mouth of an officer of the Scotch Greys.

Whilst the Greys were advancing through a shower of missiles, which knocked them about like ninepins in a bowling green, Major Clarke, one of the officers, addressing the comrade next him, made this inquiry:

"How many minutes have we yet on earth, Chesney?"*

"Three, at the very utmost, I should say," returned the other. "Nay, perhaps not one."

The next moment they were upon the enemy: and minutes, hours, and death itself were forgotten in the scene of slaughter which ensued.

Both these officers survived the battle; one (afterwards Colonel Clarke) told me he had five horses shot under him. The desperate bravery of the Scotch Greys was indeed subject of comment and admiration, even amongst the French, long after the battle.

---

* Then Lieutenant Chesney, Scotch Greys.

Anecdote of Corunna

I have been told, by one who stood by in the field and looked upon the sight as he leant upon his musket for a few minutes during the battle of Corunna, that nothing could be more affecting than the sight of Sir John Moore as he was carried off the field.

Six splendid-looking Highlanders in their picturesque costume (their mouths black with gunpowder, their marked features bearing a stern yet sorrowful expression, the dark plumes of their bonnets waving mournfully to their steps) bore him in a blanket past the soldier. To the rear a spring-cart was brought up as they slowly moved on, but the High-landers would not consent to their wounded commander being placed in it.

"We can carry him more gently ourselves," they said; "and by keeping step carefully, there will be less motion."

In this way (the blanket soaked with blood) they bore their agonized burden to the rear. Sir John, while he was being thus carried, I understand, expressed great anxiety about Sir Arthur Paget. He seemed to wish to look on that chivalrous officer before he died, and to take a last farewell of him.

"Where is Paget?" he inquired; "where is Paget?"

The soldier who gave me a description of the scene, a

grenadier of the 50th, gave me also an anecdote of one of his officers, Captain Cluny, who commanded the grenadier company of that regiment. This officer carried a heavy stick in his hand, and whilst the fire was very fierce, he saw, immediately in front, a party of the enemy, lying *perdue* behind a sort of turf battery they had thrown up. Dashing at the spot, he sprung over the impediment, and (being a powerful man, more than six feet in height) he laid about him with such amazing strength and resolution, that in a few minutes he had either stricken down or captured the whole party—six in number; and this, too, without drawing his sword. He had, indeed, beaten them to his heart's content with his heavy stick, and on some of his men coming up, the whole were handed over to them and secured.

Captain Percival of the Rifles
in the Pyrenees

Captain Percival belonged to the 3rd battalion of the Rifle Corps; he was, I think, either nephew or brother to the Percival who was shot by Bellingham. He was skirmishing in the Pyrenees, and a ball struck him in the hand.

"They are giving me something in hand, my lads, at any rate," he observed, as he bandaged the wound.

A sergeant ran up to assist him—whilst doing so, a ball hit the Captain's other hand.

"Well," he said, " they have crippled me *indeed* now."

As they were engaged tying up the second wound, a third bullet struck him in the thigh, and he fell. Two or three men carried him away to find a surgeon, and in the bustle they got amongst the French, and all were taken prisoners.

The man who told me this, was the soldier who assisted Percival. He said he was a glorious fellow. The same man was, I think, afterwards his coachman in England when the war was over.

A Presentiment

During the heat of battle at Waterloo, one of the English cavalry generals, as well known in the fashionable world for the elegance of his style and manner as for his dashing bravery in the field, just before giving the word to charge, observed an officer near him looking very dejected.

"How now, major?" said he. "Why you look as dismal as if you expected a dun at your elbow!"

"Ah!" sighed the officer, who had only recently been married, "I am thinking of my poor wife, whom I left at Brussels."

"Pooh!" said the general laughing, "thinking of your wife indeed! Why didn't you leave her in London, where I have left all my wives?"

The next minute the gallant general gave the word to his brigade to charge; and dashing at the enemy's cuirassiers, they were instantly in the midst of the dreadful conflict.

It was afterwards remembered by one who survived that charge that the newly-married officer was the first man killed.

The Marquis of Anglesey's Leg

Just as the surgeon had cut off the Marquis of Anglesey's leg in a small cottage in the village of Waterloo, Sir Hussey Vivian came into the room.

"Vivian," said the gallant soldier, "take a look at that leg," pointing to the newly-severed limb, "and tell me what you think of it. Some time hence, perhaps, I may be inclined to imagine it might have been saved, and I should like your opinion upon it."

Sir Hussey looked carefully at the shattered limb, and soon set the mind of the marquis at rest regarding it.

A large shot had gone through the knee joint, and made a terrible-looking wound.

The Field Services of the
Rifle Brigade from its
Formation to Waterloo

The Field Services of the Rifle Brigade from its Formation to Waterloo

This regiment was gazetted on the 25th of August, 1800, as the 95th Rifle Corps; but, some little time previous to this, it was considered as an *experimental corps;* and in its infancy it accompanied the expedition to Ferrol, commanded by Sir James Pulteney.

It was next engaged in the battle of Copenhagen, fought between the British fleet, under Lord Nelson, and the Danish fleet and batteries. In this sanguinary conflict the Rifle Corps lost many of its members.

In 1805, the corps composed a part of the force sent to Germany to co-operate with some of the continental troops against the French; but the expedition returned to England after a short absence, having effected nothing very material.

In the same year a second battalion was added to the 95th Rifle Corps.

In 1806, three companies of the second battalion were sent to South America, with the expedition commanded by Sir Samuel Achmuty; and five companies of the first battalion went with the expedition against Buenos Ayres, commanded by General Whitelock.

The corps was employed in the siege and storming of Monte Video, and it was engaged likewise in a warm action near Colonia, and in other affairs of minor importance.

Sir Samuel Achmuty mentioned them in very handsome terms several times.

It was engaged again in a sharp action with the Spanish troops sent out from Buenos Ayres to check the British advanced guard, which was formed by five companies of the first battalion of the Rifle Corps, and some light companies.

The advanced guard drove the Spaniards before them in gallant style, charging and capturing some field artillery from them.

In the attack on the city of Buenos Ayres, the Rifle Corps sustained a very severe loss in both officers and men. Eight companies of the regiment were present on that occasion; the remainder of the two battalions being employed the same year (1807) in the expedition to Denmark, under Lord Cathcart. The whole of the Danish fleet was taken possession of and brought to England, and a considerable part of the Capital was destroyed by bombardment.

In the spring of 1808 a part of the first battalion of the regiment was sent with an expedition to Sweden, commanded by Sir John Moore; but, in consequence of some misunderstanding between the British commander and the Swedish government, the troops did not disembark.

The same summer four hundred men of the second battalion accompanied the expedition to Portugal, commanded by Sir Arthur Wellesley; and its first encounter with the French was near Obidos. Lieutenant Bunbury was killed; and he was the first British officer that fell in the Peninsular war.

The French had a considerable quantity of cattle, which were turned out to graze near the ramparts, under the protection of the guns. Lord Wellington's intention being to reduce the place by famine, some companies of the Rifle Corps were frequently employed to approach as near as possible to the walls, and to endeavour to shoot the cattle. This always brought a cannonade on them.

The first battalion of the corps, together with a part of the second and third, were soon afterwards engaged in the battle of Fuentes d'Onoro, in which Massena's army was completely beaten and obliged to abandon its design of raising the blockade of Almeida. The regularity and steadiness evinced by the light division, when ordered to fall back in squares, during the battle of Fuentes d'Onoro, over a plain, followed by a large force of French cavalry, and heavily cannonaded at the same time, is still fresh in the recollection of some few who were present on that day.

When Lord Wellington's army was falling back from the position near Fuente Guinaldo, towards Soito, in consequence of the very superior numbers brought against it by Marshal Marmont, the Rifle Corps had a brush with some French chasseurs; a part of whom dismounted and attacked the British rear guard as light infantry. They were soon checked, and, during the remainder of that day, kept at a more respectful distance.

A short time previous to this affair, five companies of the third battalion of the regiment, under the command of Lieutenant Colonel Andrew Barnard, joined the light division from Cadiz.

Next followed the siege and storming of Ciudad Rodrigo, in which the Rifle Corps had its full share.

A detachment of the corps (together with detachments from the other regiments of the light division) was employed in the assault of an outwork near Ciudad Rodrigo. Lieutetant Colonel Colborne, of the 52nd regiment, commanded this party, which carried the works very gallantly and with great rapidity. This took place the first night of the investment of the fortress.

During the siege and storming of Badajoz, the three battalions of the regiment sustained an exceedingly heavy loss in officers and men. A detachment of the corps was also employed in the assault of Fort Piccurina, an outwork of Badajoz.

In the action which took place near Castrejon, the regiment again encountered the enemy. On this occasion the fourth and light divisions, together with several regiments of cavalry, and some horse artillery, were, for a length of time, under a very heavy cannonade. Several charges of cavalry took place, and some of the riflemen and light infantry were warmly engaged. Whilst this force was in the act of falling back over the plains to reach a position on the opposite bank of the Guarena, it was closely followed by the mass of Marmont's army, which, with vastly superior numbers, threatened to crush and overwhelm their opponents. The retreat to the river was, however, effected in beautiful order, and the British forded it under a cannonade from the heights which overlook it. The heat was intense to a degree; and the troops being unable to procure a drop of water to quench their intolerable thirst, until they reached the river, many (particularly of the Portuguese) expired for want of it; and many others fell by the roadside, and, consequently, were made prisoners by the enemy's cavalry, which pressed on with all haste in the track of the British.

On the day following, the Rifle Corps was again briskly cannonaded during the march of the light division along the Guarena, in a parallel line with the French; both armies directing their steps towards the river Tormes.

The light division was engaged, but slightly, towards evening, in the battle of Salamanca. Four divisions of the army; viz., 3rd, 4th, 5th, and 6th, with some regiments of cavalry, principally gained this glorious victory. The 2nd division was absent in the south of Portugal, under Sir Rowland Hill's command; the 1st and light divisions towards the left of the British position; and the 7th division not seriously engaged.

The Rifle Corps was next engaged with Marshal Soult's advanced guard, previous to, and during, the passage of the river Huebra, near San Munos, by the light division, which formed the rear guard during the retreat of the British army from Salamanca to Ciudad Rodrigo, in November, 1812, after the two wings of Lord Wellington's army had formed a junction at Salamanca—one wing from before Burgos, the other from Madrid.

A company of the second battalion of the regiment was sent from Cadiz with the little expedition to Tarifa, and it was actively engaged in all the operations which took place, and in the defence of the town when it was stormed by the French. The enemy suffered a heavy loss, and were so completely beaten as to be obliged to raise the siege, and to make a hasty retreat from before the place.

In the retreat of the French from before Cadiz, after they had been compelled to raise the siege in consequence of the battle of Salamanca, a part of the second battalion of the Rifle Corps was engaged with their rear guard near Seville, and it was mentioned in complimentary terms by the officer commanding on that occasion.

In the defence of the bridge of Aranjuez, a part of the second battalion aided materially, by its well-directed fire, in stopping the enemy in his attempt at passing.

During the remainder of the war in the Peninsula, the first battalion consisted of *six* companies only; its losses on various occasions having so reduced its ranks (notwithstanding reinforcements frequently sent out from England) that six companies were all that could be kept effective. The second battalion had also *six* companies, and the third battalion *five:* all of those were in the light division. The remainder of the corps was at its depot, at Shorncliffe, in Kent, and was composed of a few worn-out men and recruits.

Near the village of San Millan, on the north bank of the Ebro, the three battalions of the regiment took a very prominent part in the attack and complete defeat of a French division of infantry, which was surprised in mid-day by the light division. The enemy lost many in killed, wounded, and prisoners, and the greater part of their baggage was captured. Some hundreds sought refuge in the mountains.

Three days afterwards, the three battalions were warmly engaged in the glorious battle of Vittoria. The French lost the whole of their baggage and their military chest, one hundred and fifty-one pieces of artillery, many prisoners, and many killed and wounded. This signal defeat obliged the French to retreat at once into their own country. During the 23rd and 24th of June, the first and third battalions of the Rifle Corps were constantly in close pursuit of the French rear guard, and frequently engaged. On the latter day they aided in capturing a howitzer, not far from Pampluna. From the heights of Santa Barbara, in the Pyrenees, near the town of Vera, the first battalion next drove the French pickets, whilst, at the same moment, the 43rd regiment was engaged amongst the enclosures near that town.

The corps was engaged again near the bridge of Yanci, on the Bidassoa, with Soult's rear guard, which was in full retreat for the passes of Vera and Echelar, after the brilliant victory obtained by the right wing of the British army, a few days before, near Pampluna. A destructive fire, from the riflemen of the light division, threw the fugitives into great disorder; many threw away their arms and knapsacks, and scrambled up the face of a rough mountain on the right bank of the Bidassoa, leaving a quantity of baggage in the hands of their pursuers. A regiment of French lancers, which was in the enemy's rear guard, fared but badly on this occasion; for, being unable to retaliate with their lances in the rough and mountainous road which runs parallel with the Bidassoa, they got into a sad plight, and, throwing away their lances, and abandoning many of their horses, sought refuge in the mountains.

On the following day, the first and third battalions of the regiment attacked and drove from one of the rocky mountains in the Pyrenees, several battalions of French infantry, which were obliged to seek refuge in France without delay. The 43rd regiment supported the riflemen in this attack.

A detachment of the Rifle Corps, under the command of a subaltern, was sent to take a part in the storming of San Sebastian, the light division having received orders to send some men from each of its regiments. This detachment suffered very severely, in common with the other troops employed in that bloody and obstinately contested business. The same day on which the assault of San Sebastian took place, a large French force forded the Bidassoa, near Vera, which brought it in contact with the light division. The second battalion of the Rifle Corps was a good deal engaged in and about the churchyard and outbuildings of Vera; and the gallant and obstinate defence which was made, the same night, by two companies of the second battalion at the bridge, is particularly deserving of being recorded. This small force could not stop some thousand Frenchmen, but it caused them a terrible loss.

About this period all the effective men that could be

scraped together at the depot in England were sent to Belgium, and constituted a part of the force under Sir Thomas Graham, that officer having been replaced in the Peninsular army by Sir John Hope. This detachment of the corps (amounting to three companies) was warmly engaged in an action with the French at Merxem, in the vicinity of Antwerp; and it was likewise engaged in affairs of lesser importance in that country.

The three battalions were next engaged in a desperate attack made by the light division on a formidable entrenched position in the pass of Vera. The third battalion of the regiment commenced the business of the day by driving from a mountain an advanced party of the French, and this was followed by a general advance of the light division against the entrenched position. After a sharp conflict the enemy was driven from his strong ground; and the second brigade of the light division, which Colonel Colborne, of the 52nd regiment, commanded on that day (composed of the 52nd regiment, the second battalion of the Rifle Corps, and the first Portuguese light infantry), suffered very severely, and exhibited great gallantry and good conduct in forcing the different entrenchments with the bayonet.

A few weeks after this, the three battalions of the corps had an ample share in the battle of the Nivelle; on which day the British army was established on the soil of France, and Marshal Soult was obliged to retreat to a strong entrenched camp near Bayonne.

In a close reconnaissance, made by the left wing of the army, under Sir John Hope's command, on the French entrenched camp near Bayonne, the Rifle Corps was soon afterwards engaged, as likewise in several minor affairs of posts, between Arcanguez and Bayonne.

In the battles of the Nive, which lasted five days, and

consisted of different attacks on various points of our extended line of defence, the Rifle Corps had its share.

The second and third battalions were in the battle of Orthes; the first battalion, having been sent a short time before to St. Jean de Luz to get its new clothing, was unavoidably prevented from taking a share in that action, which threw additional lustre on the British arms.

The three battalions of the regiment were shortly afterwards very hotly engaged at Tarbes, on the Adour, driving the enemy from a ridge of formidable heights, and inflicting on them a heavy loss in an extremely short space of time. Eleven officers of the corps were killed and wounded in this short but sharp action.

In following the French rear-guard towards Toulouse, the third battalion had an affair near the village of Tournfuelle.

In the battle of Toulouse, which followed shortly afterwards, the three battalions of the corps were engaged. This battle terminated the war in the Peninsula, which commenced (as far as the British army was concerned) on the 1st day of August, 1808, and ended on the 10th of April, 1814.

On the return of the army from Bordeaux to England, five companies of the third battalion were sent with the expedition against New Orleans, in the various operations against which place it suffered very severely indeed. The first and second battalions were also under orders to embark for America early in the ensuing spring, but Napoleon's escape from Elba changed their destination to Flanders.

The gallantry displayed by a company of the third battalion, commanded by Captain Hallen, which formed the advance picket on the first night, the troops, under Sir John Keane, landed on the banks of the Mississippi (when it was vigorously attacked by an overwhelming body of Americans); and the obstinacy with which this little band defended the post entrusted to their charge, should be recorded as an affair of posts but rarely equalled, and never surpassed in devoted bravery.

Had the expedition terminated more favourably, it is presumed that the brave commander of that company would not have gone unrewarded.

The first battalion of the corps being in Sir Thomas Picton's division, was engaged in the battle of Quatre Bras.

The first and second battalions, as well as that part of the third which was not with the New Orleans expedition, were hotly engaged throughout the glorious day of Waterloo. Their losses were exceedingly severe.

From the formation of the regiment in 1800 to the day of Waterloo, it appears it has been engaged with the enemy, as follows:

In one great naval battle (Copenhagen)

In three sieges and storms (Monte Video, Ciudad Rodrigo, and Badajoz)

In the attack of Buenos Ayres, under General Whitelock

In the assault of the American lines at New Orleans

A detachment sent to assist in the defence of Tarifa

A detachment sent to assist in the storming of San Sebastian

In eleven hotly contested actions not termed *general* ones

In thirteen general actions

In the battle of Quatre Bras, which was fought principally by Sir Thomas Picton's division, and is not termed a general action

And in upwards of forty minor actions, affairs of posts, reconnaissances, &c, &c, many of which were very-severe.

With the exception of the expedition to Ferrol, and the battle of Copenhagen, under Lord Nelson, the whole of the above-mentioned services were performed between the early part of the year 1807, and the month of June, 1815, a period of but little more than eight years.

In conclusion, it should be remarked, that although most of the effective men of the whole corps were sent to the Peninsula, and that the three battalions were in the field, neither of them could be supplied with reinforcements from the depot in sufficient numbers to fill up their constant losses.

It has already been stated, that in the spring of 1810 the first battalion was reduced from *ten* to *eight* companies; and after the sieges and storms of Ciudad Rodrigo and Badajoz, it was reduced to *six* companies; from which period, up to and including the battles of Quatre Bras and Waterloo, it consisted of only that number.

The second battalion could not either be furnished with men sufficiently fast to keep it up to more than *six* companies; and the third battalion had but *five* companies in the Peninsula.

The recruiting at home was attended with as much success as that of other regiments, and more so than that of most. The best proof of it is, that on the return of the two battalions from Corunna and Vigo, in January, 1809, a third battalion was formed in a few days by volunteers from various militia regiments; and the number of men obtained, in that extremely short space of time, exceeded very considerably one thousand.

If, then, it is asked how came it to pass that the three battalions could not be kept up to their proper complement in the field, the answer is obvious, and will be found in the perusal of the foregoing sketch of its services.

It will there be seen, that it was not only employed in general actions, sieges, and storms, in common with regiments of the line; but that the very numerous *affairs* (as they are termed) in which, as a matter of course, it was constantly engaged, owing to the peculiar nature of its service, caused an unceasing drain on its strength, from which the regiments of the line were comparatively exempt.

The best test of the correctness of this assertion would be found in the returns of officers and soldiers of the 95th Rifle Corps killed and wounded in that manner.

In looking over the returns in the Gazette of the losses sustained by different regiments in various battles, those who are not properly informed on the subject would very naturally conclude that the battalions of the Rifle Corps amounted to *ten* companies each in the field, and would judge of their losses accordingly, whereas a very false estimate would thus be made.

For example:—at the sieges and storms of Ciudad Rodrigo and Badajoz, instead of three battalions, of *ten* companies each, there were only *fifteen* altogether; viz., eight of the first, two of the second, and five of the third; and in every action which took place from that time, up to the termination of the Peninsular war at Toulouse, there were but *seventeen* companies in that country; that is, only *two* companies more than one complete battalion and a half.

At Waterloo there were but *fourteen* companies of the corps; viz., six of the first, six of the second, and two of the third battalion; yet, persons uninformed on the subject would suppose, on seeing the returns of killed and wounded after different actions, that the three battalions consisted (like those of other regiments) of *ten* companies each, having thirty captains, sixty first-lieutenants, and thirty second-lieutenants, with field-officers and adjutants in proportion.

This supposition would, indeed, be most erroneous, as not more than half that number were in the field.

In looking, therefore, at the losses of each battalion, due regard should be paid to those facts; and it should be borne in mind, that a battalion, composed of *five* companies, losing *fifty* men, is tantamount to one of *ten* companies losing *one hundred*.

I regret exceedingly that I am not in possession of returns of the losses sustained by my old corps in its numerous actions with the enemy, and by sickness. Such a document would have, perhaps, but few (if any) parallels in the service; and it would be seen, moreover, that the Peninsular army had other formidable enemies to contend with besides the sword, in the form of pestilential fevers, agues, &c. &c.

Although many pleasurable feelings have been experienced, by thus calling to mind occurrences long since passed, and which are, in all probability, nearly effaced from the memory of most, those feelings are not unalloyed by reflecting, how very, very few, now remain of those who participated with me in those spirit stirring scenes.

Jonathan Leach
Lieutenant-Colonel

LEONAUR

ALSO FROM LEONAUR

AVAILABLE IN SOFTCOVER OR HARDCOVER WITH DUST JACKET

CAPTAIN OF THE 95th (Rifles) *by Jonathan Leach*—An officer of Wellington's Sharpshooters during the Peninsular, South of France and Waterloo Campaigns of the Napoleonic Wars.

BUGLER AND OFFICER OF THE RIFLES *by William Green & Harry Smith* With the 95th (Rifles) during the Peninsular & Waterloo Campaigns of the Napoleonic Wars

BAYONETS, BUGLES AND BONNETS *by James 'Thomas' Todd*—Experiences of hard soldiering with the 71st Foot - the Highland Light Infantry - through many battles of the Napoleonic wars including the Peninsular & Waterloo Campaigns

THE ADVENTURES OF A LIGHT DRAGOON *by George Farmer & G.R. Gleig*—A cavalryman during the Peninsular & Waterloo Campaigns, in captivity & at the siege of Bhurtpore, India

THE COMPLEAT RIFLEMAN HARRIS *by Benjamin Harris as told to & transcribed by Captain Henry Curling*—The adventures of a soldier of the 95th (Rifles) during the Peninsular Campaign of the Napoleonic Wars

WITH WELLINGTON'S LIGHT CAVALRY *by William Tomkinson*—The Experiences of an officer of the 16th Light Dragoons in the Peninsular and Waterloo campaigns of the Napoleonic Wars.

SURTEES OF THE RIFLES *by William Surtees*—A Soldier of the 95th (Rifles) in the Peninsular campaign of the Napoleonic Wars.

ENSIGN BELL IN THE PENINSULAR WAR *by George Bell*—The Experiences of a young British Soldier of the 34th Regiment 'The Cumberland Gentlemen' in the Napoleonic wars.

WITH THE LIGHT DIVISION *by John H. Cooke*—The Experiences of an Officer of the 43rd Light Infantry in the Peninsula and South of France During the Napoleonic Wars

NAPOLEON'S IMPERIAL GUARD: FROM MARENGO TO WATERLOO *by J. T. Headley*—This is the story of Napoleon's Imperial Guard from the bearskin caps of the grenadiers to the flamboyance of their mounted chasseurs, their principal characters and the men who commanded them.

BATTLES & SIEGES OF THE PENINSULAR WAR *by W. H. Fitchett*—Corunna, Busaco, Albuera, Ciudad Rodrigo, Badajos, Salamanca, San Sebastian & Others

LEONAUR

ALSO FROM LEONAUR
AVAILABLE IN SOFTCOVER OR HARDCOVER WITH DUST JACKET

THE JENA CAMPAIGN: 1806 by *F. N. Maude*—The Twin Battles of Jena & Auerstadt Between Napoleon's French and the Prussian Army.

PRIVATE O'NEIL by *Charles O'Neil*—The recollections of an Irish Rogue of H. M. 28th Regt.—The Slashers— during the Peninsula & Waterloo campaigns of the Napoleonic wars.

ROYAL HIGHLANDER by *James Anton*—A soldier of H.M 42nd (Royal) Highlanders during the Peninsular, South of France & Waterloo Campaigns of the Napoleonic Wars.

CAPTAIN BLAZE by *Elzéar Blaze*—Elzéar Blaze recounts his life and experiences in Napoleon's army in a well written, articulate and companionable style.

LEJEUNE VOLUME 1 by *Louis-François Lejeune*—The Napoleonic Wars through the Experiences of an Officer on Berthier's Staff.

LEJEUNE VOLUME 2 by *Louis-François Lejeune*—The Napoleonic Wars through the Experiences of an Officer on Berthier's Staff.

FUSILIER COOPER by *John S. Cooper*—Experiences in the 7th (Royal) Fusiliers During the Peninsular Campaign of the Napoleonic Wars and the American Campaign to New Orleans.

CAPTAIN COIGNET by *Jean-Roch Coignet*—A Soldier of Napoleon's Imperial Guard from the Italian Campaign to Russia and Waterloo.

FIGHTING NAPOLEON'S EMPIRE by *Joseph Anderson*—The Campaigns of a British Infantryman in Italy, Egypt, the Peninsular & the West Indies During the Napoleonic Wars.

CHASSEUR BARRES by *Jean-Baptiste Barres*—The experiences of a French Infantryman of the Imperial Guard at Austerlitz, Jena, Eylau, Friedland, in the Peninsular, Lutzen, Bautzen, Zinnwald and Hanau during the Napoleonic Wars.

MARINES TO 95TH (RIFLES) by *Thomas Fernyhough*—The military experiences of Robert Fernyough during the Napoleonic Wars.

HUSSAR ROCCA by *Albert Jean Michel de Rocca*—A French cavalry officer's experiences of the Napoleonic Wars and his views on the Peninsular Campaigns against the Spanish, British And Guerilla Armies.

SERGEANT BOURGOGNE by *Adrien Bourgogne*—With Napoleon's Imperial Guard in the Russian Campaign and on the Retreat from Moscow 1812 - 13.

Printed in the United Kingdom
by Lightning Source UK Ltd.
126503UK00001B/48/A